A WOMEN'S BIBLE STUDY ON THE LIFE OF PETER

Perfectly FLAWED

God Transforms Our Weaknesses into Strengths

LISA TONEY

Abingdon Women | Nashville

Perfectly Flawed

God Transforms Our Weaknesses into Strengths

Copyright © 2025 Lisa Toney

All rights reserved.

978-17910-3254-8

MANUFACTURED IN THE UNITED STATES OF AMERICA

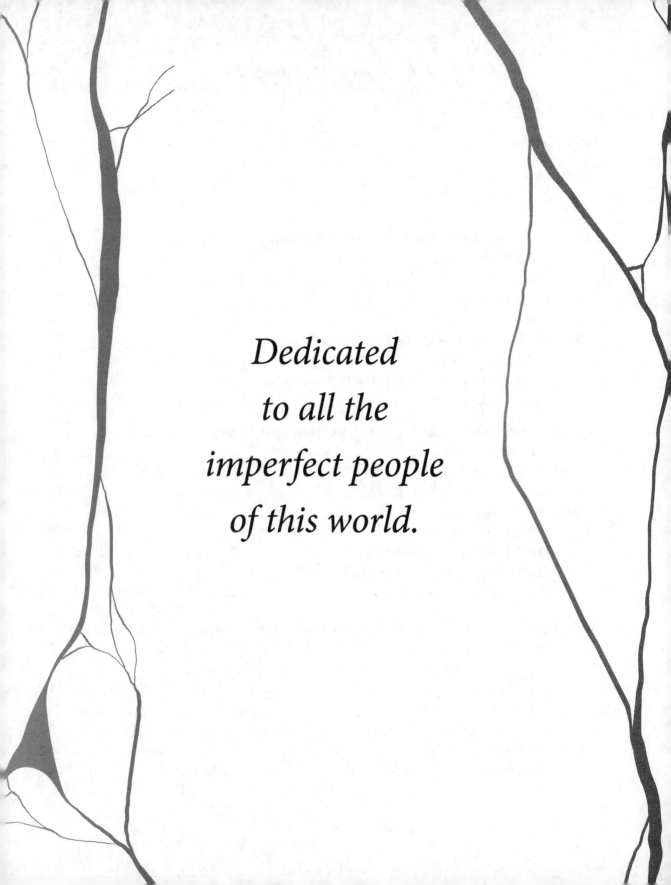

*Dedicated
to all the
imperfect people
of this world.*

Contents

About the Author

Hello, I'm Lisa.

"For **THIS,** we have Jesus."

This is my battle cry. In every situation, it seems to apply. Jesus makes all the difference in the world.

Every morning, I am shocked, overjoyed, humbled, and bursting with gratitude. Out of this overflow, I love to speak and write about ways to build easy, intentional, and powerful faith habits to live for Jesus. As a professor and pastor, I love to help people answer the "why" behind the faith habits I teach.

I've listened, learned, taught, and served alongside the church for more than twenty years. As the CEO of Faith Habits, my joy is to provide faith-based classes, coaching, and resources to encourage engagement with God.

With a master's in divinity from Fuller Theological Seminary and a communications degree from Taylor University, my passions are faith and communication. Partnering with Women of Faith, Aspire Women's Events, and Guideposts are some of the super fun opportunities God has brought my way.

In addition to this study, I have authored the projects *Thrive: Live Like You Matter, The Scripture Challenge,* and The Wholehearted Psalms Devotion series.

After growing up in the Midwest, I discovered I'm solar-powered and now live in Southern California with my husband, four kids, a puppy, a gecko, and five chickens. My husband and I often lead faith-based group tours of the Bible lands (Israel, Greece, Italy, Turkey, etc.) with InspireTravelGroup.org and walk where the unstoppable, incomparable, life-changing movement of Jesus began.

Let's be friends!

 LisaToneyLife

 LisaToneyLife

 YouTube Lisa Toney

 lisatoney.com

Foreword

I first met Lisa Toney at a Women of Faith event and immediately knew she was something special. She was full of the joy of the Lord. She dressed funky, had cool hair and a giant smile. I thought, well, *who is this?* Little did I know this would be the beginning of a beautiful friendship.

As a sister in Christ and powerful proclaimer of God's Word, Lisa journeys alongside Women of Faith and uses her teaching gift to speak into the lives of thousands of women. What a blessing to see women's hearts and lives changed as they dig deeply into Scripture and discover how much they are known, seen, and loved by Jesus.

Lisa has a way of making biblical truths come alive with fun stories and really helpful strategies for living out faith habits. I am so excited that her *Perfectly Flawed* Bible study is about the disciple Peter—because we can all relate to him. Every time he puts his foot in his mouth, I think that could have been me, oh so easily.

As I mentor and coach thousands of women worldwide through Women of Faith, I have seen firsthand how women deeply struggle with perfectionism. Most of us long to be perfect because we want to be accepted. We hate to admit that we don't know something or need help. Lisa's Bible study comes at a crucial time, as we are facing an unprecedented mental health crisis. There is great hope in Jesus, and *Perfectly Flawed* walks us through an encounter with Jesus through Peter's eyes. Peter messed up often and repeatedly, and Jesus kept him around. He kept coaching and mentoring him to prepare Peter to launch Christianity in the nations. Jesus is powerful enough to transform our weaknesses into strengths to be used for His glory.

You are going to enjoy *Perfectly Flawed* so much. I know you, too, will become fast friends with Lisa. Jump on in with both feet and stay the course. You will learn a whole lot, be challenged, and grow deeper in love with the Jesus who called Peter out upon the water. He may just invite you too to do things you could never imagine.

Alita Reynolds
President, Women of Faith

About This Study

Well, hey there, friend. I'm so glad that you picked up this Bible study.

I am excited to dive into this with you, and I have to confess something to you right off the bat. Can I be super honest with you? Peter is my fav. This guy jumps off the pages when I read about him walking with Jesus. Is it bad to have a favorite disciple?

Maybe we just hear more about him than some of the others. Each of the twelve Jesus chose was called and vitally important to His leadership team. I'm thankful for them all; we can learn from each one. But Peter has a special place in my heart. He was passionate and headstrong, often confused, made mistakes, ran fast, spoke boldly, and loved Jesus deeply. I think all that energy and passion is exhilarating and contagious. I want to follow Jesus with that kind of zealous fervor. To see Jesus through his eyes. That is what this Bible study is about. It's about looking at Jesus through the eyes of Peter.

These daily studies will help you fight against all the shiny distractions out there. Get out your Bible and a pen, carve out some time each day, and curl up in a cozy place to read through the passages and answer the questions. The goal is to help you get to know Peter and Jesus in a deeper way. You get to hang out with them and spend some time. Allow their stories, accounts, and teachings to pass through your eyeballs and shape your thinking, relationships, and choices. That is impact. That is lasting. That is transformation.

This study is for everyone. Whether you are an experienced Bible study pro or just starting out, this study is meant to draw you closer to Jesus, to allow you to gain new knowledge and wrestle with questions about your life. I have found that what I put into a Bible study is strongly connected to what I get out of that Bible study. When I can commit to daily time with Jesus, it changes my outlook on life. Mostly it helps me start my day by getting my mindset thinking a little more like Jesus and a little less like this world. Those daily study times allow me to saturate my struggles with Jesus rather than worry.

I've also found that I love doing this with friends. Whether you gather a group together in person or online, or you join a Bible study at church or work, it is always more fun with friends. Which six to ten women would you love to hang out with for a few weeks? I love to be invited to things, don't you? Even if I can't go, I love being asked. It makes me feel valued and included. I bet if you text ten women, you'll probably get six who are excited to join you, and just like that, you've got an amazing community with whom to share your life and talk about your faith for the next six weeks.

Hey friend! I am putting together a little group for the next six weeks to do a Bible study. 📖🙏🖤✨

It's going to be so fun.💃😎📸 It's all about how God can use us in spite of our flaws! 💯

I need that encouragement; how about you? We are going to meet on (insert day) at this time (insert time) starting on (insert start date) at (insert location).✅👍

Can you join us? I'm bringing (insert fav food)! I'm excited to spend time with you and hear your heart. 🖤🤗

Here's a sample text you can use.

We need more friends in our life. We need more of Jesus. This gives you a win-win!

HOW TO USE THIS STUDY

We start each week with a power-packed, oh-so-helpful focus verse to get your mindset focused on Jesus. It will be pretty amazing to hear from your group (and share your own experience) about how God uses these focus verses to keep your head from going into the dark spaces of worry, stress, anxiety, self-doubt, self-hate, criticism, envy, and so many others.

Here is how you should interact with your focus verse each day:

- Read your focus verse.
- Say your focus verse out loud.
- Say the verse slowly and pause on phrases and words.
- Highlight and circle words that stick out to you.
- At the end of each day, practice writing out your focus verse using the memory prompts.
- See if you can say it from memory by the end of the week.

After that, choose your own path. You get to decide how you want to interact with this material. Adulting has its perks. No one is going to force you into this. Let me just say—you are *invited*. I *invite* you to rearrange your day to include this study. If you don't have time, please talk to the person who manages your time and schedule *immediately*. Oh wait, is that *you*?

Intentional time with Jesus and a faith community will absolutely help you to slow your roll, prioritize the people God has given you, and bring clarity to what the next step is that Jesus wants you to take.

I have so many flaws. My four kids, husband, coworkers, and friends could give you a list to encircle the globe a gazillion times, easily. Some days, all my inadequacies leave me questioning why God sticks with me. Do you ever ask that question?

I find it astounding that Jesus still wants to include me in Kingdom work despite all my flaws. Peter's story gives each of us that same hope. Peter was perfectly flawed and still chosen by Jesus. Likewise, even with all of our mistakes, flaws, inadequacies, and weaknesses, Jesus still chooses us.

You are still chosen, flaws and all…to follow, learn, represent, and minister in His name. It's mind-blowing, isn't it? In all the best ways.

In the next six weeks, you will get to know Peter and the Jesus he so dearly loved. Peter's flaws are sometimes easier to handle than our own. The same Jesus who remained faithful to Peter in his weakest moments remains faithful to you and me. Jesus is able, willing, and powerful enough to transform our weaknesses into strengths for His glory.

As we journey together, we will prayerfully ask the Holy Spirit to show up in mighty ways and transform our lives daily. Please join our Facebook and Instagram communities @ **perfectlyflawed** and share how you are impacted. I love hearing how Jesus speaks to you and is transforming your weaknesses into strengths.

Here is your opportunity to think through when is going to be best for you to work on your daily homework.

I plan to do my study at this time _____ a.m./p.m. on these days:

_____ M _____ T _____ W _____ Th _____ F _____ Sat _____ Sun

at this location _____ .

Write a prayer of expectation and anticipation to Jesus here:

Peter was the rock that Jesus said He wanted to found His church upon. That means Jesus wanted His church to be filled with people like Peter. People who are bold in their faith, eager to follow Jesus, and ready to wrestle down the demons of our mistakes so that we can be free.

Jesus came to bring that freedom. Despite our lousy choices, atrocious habits, and embarrassing mistakes, Jesus still chooses you. Not only does He choose you but He can also use you to do things bigger than yourself. Bigger than you've ever imagined. We aren't perfect. We are perfectly flawed. Thankfully, Jesus doesn't shutter, cringe, or bat an eye. He looks at our imperfections and says, *Bring them to me, and I can do things you never imagined possible.*

Perfectly Flawed...
Forgiven and Faithful...

Perfectly FLAWED *and* CHOSEN

(Peter Met Jesus)

FOCUS *Verse*

But you are a chosen people, a royal priesthood, a holy nation, God's special possession, that you may declare the praises of him who called you out of darkness into his wonderful light.

(1 Peter 2:9)

TAKE ACTION

Invite a friend out for coffee or lunch and let her know all the reasons you have chosen her as a friend!

Serve
At a local food pantry.

CHOSEN

Creation's Canvas

Plan a hike by yourself or with family or friends. As you hike, breathe in the fresh air and look around to see the complex ecosystems around you. How amazing is our God that He created all of that for you to enjoy! Read Psalm 8.

CREATE

Choose a photo that you have been meaning to frame, turn into a canvas, ornament, or paint. Do it!

A Word from Peter

Shalom, friends, and welcome. Simon here; you probably know me as Peter. I was given this name by the best person I've ever known, who was actually more than just a regular person. I will tell you all about Him during our time together, and honestly, I can't wait.

Jesus was…well, so many things. He was the one that my people (the Jews) had been waiting for so long. Jesus was wise. He was kind. He was funny. He was miraculous. He *changed* my life. He made me a better person. He accepted me with all my flaws. I still don't know why he chose me, but I am so glad he did. I thought I was just a regular guy, nobody special. I could not believe it when Jesus asked me to join His disciples. It was crazy. None of the other rabbis invited fishermen to join them. But Jesus was not like all the other rabbis. He was like no one I had ever seen or heard before. Well, I'll get into all of that in the days ahead. You are going to have your mind blown. I know I certainly did.

I grew up in northern Galilee in Israel. A little fishing town called Bethsaida was my home. It is on the western side of the Sea of Galilee. *Kinneret* is its Hebrew name. The sea also became known as the Sea of Tiberias when the city of Tiberias was established on the west shore in honor of the Roman emperor Tiberias.

I am from a family of fishermen. I knew those waters well. We caught mostly tilapia. They fed my family and provided a modest income as my business. A good day on the water was a daily wage, but a bad day on the water, well, let's not talk about that. I hated failure. I hated how it made me feel and how it made me look. I hated what it did to those around me who depended upon me. Ironically, Jesus was not afraid to talk about my failures and even still looked me in the eye when I failed. He never let my failures change the potential He saw in me and the influence He had planned for me. He seemed to do that with everyone, which is why Jesus was the most amazing person ever to walk this earth. That's how Jesus was during His ministry and how He was for believers throughout time. He never changes. You'll see. All that He did then continues.

Here are a few things you should know about me as we begin our journey together.

I was married, and my younger brother Andrew was the one who introduced me to Jesus. He also became a disciple of Jesus, just like me. I was the son of Jonah (or some called him John), who taught me everything I knew about fishing, boats, and the sea. Andrew, Abba, and I were part of the family fishing business. We were big-hearted, hard-headed, passion-filled, God-honoring Jewish men who worked hard to provide for our families.

ΣΊΜΩΝ, SIMŌN IN GREEK

כֵּיפָא, KEPHA, 'ROCK/STONE IN ARAMAIC

ΠΈΤΡΟΣ, PETROS, FROM THE GREEK/LATIN WORD FOR A ROCK OR STONE (PETRA)

ΣΊΜΩΝ ΠΈΤΡΟΣ (SÍMON PÉTROS, SIMON PETER) APPEARS 19 TIMES IN THE NEW TESTAMENT

My given name was Simon, from the Hebrew word שִׁמְעוֹן (Šim'ôn), meaning "to listen" or "to hear." It was a pretty common name around here. Nothing special, really. It was meant to remind me to take in any knowledge I was given along life's journey. I didn't always do that. I did try, but I confess I was not much known for my patience. I made quick decisions about some things . . . okay, maybe most things.

I met Jesus, and He changed my life. Despite all my mistakes and failures, Jesus wanted me with Him. He still chose me and allowed me the honor of serving alongside Him. I'm still in awe of that. I never thought this fisherman would leave his boat to follow a man like Jesus. He made me bold in ways I never expected.

Jesus has a way of transforming weaknesses into surprising strengths for His glory. He did it for me, and He can do it for you.

Shalom,

Simon Peter

DAY 1: UNFURLING THE SAILS

Awkward. Sometimes, meeting people can be awkward. I love meeting new people and hearing their stories. Our stories are what connect us. But every once in a while, there is just an awkward moment. Have you ever gone to shake someone's hand, and they went in for the hug? Or the other way around? You went for the hug, and they offered the handshake. *Awkward.*

Listening to a morning news podcast, I heard about a man who got locked out of his hotel room and had to go down to the front desk to get a new room key. *Naked.* He thought he was walking into the bathroom, but instead, he walked out into the hallway, and the door shut behind him. I bet that was an introduction the reception desk worker won't forget. *Awkward.*

Introductions can be robotic and forgetful or...a gateway to a life change. I met my husband in a Greek class at Fuller Seminary. He likes to tell people I asked for his phone number first. Which I did...then I asked for the phone numbers of the rest of our small group too. I had no idea when I first met him that we would end up married!

What introduction do you remember as being very meaningful (or just kinda crazy like Greek class) in your life?

Today, we begin our introduction to Peter. He was called by Jesus to be one of His twelve disciples. The disciples were the students of Jesus who later became His representatives, challenged to spread the word of His life and ministry.

Look up John 1:41-42. Who introduced Peter to Jesus? What did Peter's brother believe to be true about Jesus?

What did Jesus know about Peter as soon as he saw him?

Cephas is Aramaic, and Peter is Greek—both mean *rock*. Peter is the *rock* star disciple. See what I did there? Fair warning: I love puns.

In Peter's time, a rabbi was not a formal leader of a synagogue or even a religious community. Rather, rabbis taught people how to live Torah (the first five books of the Old Testament). *Rabbi* was more of an honorary title. Rabbis would teach the Scriptures, interpret them, and invite students to follow and learn their ways. A student, or disciple, would follow the rabbi and learn his particular way of teaching and interpreting Scripture.

The Pharisees and Sadducees were both religious groups within Judaism during the time of Jesus. Both groups loved the law but interpreted it differently. The Sadducees were more wealthy, aristocratic, conservative, literal in their interpretations of the law, closely connected to the temple, and controlled the majority of the seats in the Sanhedrin. The Pharisees gave oral tradition equal authority to the written law, controlled the synagogues, and were more representative of and respected by the working people. The Sanhedrin was the seventy-member ruling court of Israel that comprised both Sadducees and Pharisees. The Pharisees were considered rabbis. Sadducees were not. Most Sadducees were priests in the temple, but not all of them. Rabbis were religious teachers who served in synagogues. Priests were descendants of Aaron and worked in the temple in Jerusalem.

The Mishna is a reliable historical source that describes the educational process for a Jewish boy in the time of Jesus. The Mishna is filled with the rabbinic interpretations of Scripture written during the second century AD. Jewish scholars believe it contains the oral tradition used from the first century BC to the first century AD. Thus, it gives us helpful insight into what happened during Jesus's lifetime.

At five years old [one is fit] for the Scripture; at ten years, the Mishna (oral Torah, interpretations) at thirteen for the fulfilling of the commandments; at fifteen, the Talmud (making Rabbinic interpretations) at eighteen, the bride-chamber, at twenty pursuing a vocation, at thirty for authority (able to teach others).[1]

Jesus began his ministry when He turned thirty and began to call disciples. The vocation of a rabbi was to be a spiritual leader. Jesus grew up with his earthly father, Joseph, as a carpenter. Likely, He followed in his footsteps and learned that trade. When He began his public ministry, it surprised those who had known his family while Jesus grew up in Nazareth. Jesus became a wandering itinerant rabbi who had not gone the traditional route of becoming a rabbi. Rabbis were deeply respected, and it was considered a tremendous honor to be a student of a famous rabbi. Jesus was not famous when he called His disciples. He was not known at all.

Read John 1:35-42.

Read Mark 1:29-31. Who is mentioned as being related to Peter?

Whom does that imply was also in Peter's life, although not specifically mentioned?

We don't know if Peter's wife was still alive during the writing of the Gospels or if Peter was widowed, but there was definitely a *Mrs.* Peter at some point. There may have also been some mini-mes, but we don't have a record of the births of the tiny humans. All the other disciples, as far as we know, were single. Simon Peter was the only disciple we know was married.

Let's look at some more of Peter's family, starting with his brother Andrew.

Reread John 1:35-42.

What are the two things Andrew did after he met Jesus?

1.

2.

Everything changed for Peter when he was introduced to Jesus. That is the power of the presence of Jesus.

Just like Andrew brought Simon Peter to Jesus, we will spend time in this study with Peter and let him bring us to Jesus. *Everything* changed for Peter when he was introduced to Jesus. That is the power of the presence of Jesus. That is the power we are invited into. The power of Jesus can heal, restore, and resurrect dead things. It is an unparalleled power that can refresh, renew, and re-engage our hearts. A power that can give us a fresh perspective, identity, hope, and purpose. Sound good? Oh yeah.

What do you *need* from the power of the presence of Jesus right now?

Look up these passages about being in God's presence.

- Exodus 33:14
- Psalm 16:11
- Psalm 89:15
- Psalm 140:30
- Acts 30:20-21

Write out the one that speaks to you most right now. What is the Holy Spirit prompting in your heart?

What do these passages promise and teach us about being in God's presence?

Like an embrace that leaves you smelling like a powerful perfume that you did not apply, the people we hang around rub off on us. They can leave a delicious aroma you adore or stink worse than abandoned fish rotting in the sun. The people you let fill your brain and heart shape you.

People sometimes influence us in surprising ways. Whenever we choose a podcast to play, a show to watch, a movie to see, a book to read, a sermon to listen to, or a class to take, we absorb what they are saying and doing like a sponge in the water. We process and filter that information. Sifting through it, we select what we like. We adopt words, mannerisms, and ideas.

One of the greatest faith habits you can cultivate is that of discernment, so that you can make wise choices about who can and should speak into your life. Even the most fruit-filled (Galatians 5:22-23) spiritual superhuman will never get it right 100 percent of the time. Only Jesus can—which is why we want more of Him for every need, hurt, and emotion that leaves us spinning out, wondering what is right-side-up. For *this*, we have Jesus, my friends. We will journey with Peter each day and watch Jesus transform his weaknesses into strengths—knowing that He can do the same for us.

Worship with Chris Tomlin as he sings "Jesus."

Peter had the best introduction ever to Jesus. He had often unfurled the sails on his boat to start a new day, but now the sails were unfurled for a new adventure with Jesus.

Worship the one Peter met as we set sail on our journey with him. Open the camera app on your phone and hover over this QR code. When the link pops up, click it.

WEEK 1 FOCUS VERSE: LEARN IT AND LIVE IT.

Try filling in the blanks to help you learn the verse. You can look back if you need some help. Practice each day, and pretty soon you will have it. The Holy Spirit will activate it in your head and heart right when you need to hear from God most.

But you are a _____ people, a _____ priesthood, a _____ nation, God's special _____, that you may _____ the _____ of him who _____ you out of _____ into his wonderful _____.

(1 Peter 2:9)

DAY 2: UNEXPECTED CATCH

It was epic. I was leaving. Adventuring. Making a change. Rolling out. The tide was turning.

Moving across the country from Michigan to California was exciting and scary, all rolled into one big bag of adventure. One of the fun parts was staying with different friends along my route to Fuller Seminary in Pasadena, California. The scary part was that I had only enough money for one semester of school. It was a big faith move. When my traveling buddy had to fly home when we reached Colorado, I had to drive solo the rest of the way. I was out of friends to stay with too.

I rolled into Las Vegas as evening came. Everyone had told me to stay in Vegas because it was so cheap. That was exactly my budget. After leaving one huge casino that was anything but cheap, I ended up staring at a motel with a flashing vacancy sign. The price matched my wallet, so I stayed. It was sketchy at best.

I promptly moved all the room furniture that I could shove in front of the door for extra security. Sleeping with one eye open, I was up before the sun.

As I got to my Blazer, I discovered some sneaky ninjas had lightened my load and stolen my car top carrier filled with my treasures. Spending the morning in the Vegas police station was not part of my schedule for the day. Well, you know what they say...*what drives into Vegas stays in Vegas.* Or something like that. Leaving Sin City, I drove the rest of the way to California, a little emptier than expected.

Have you ever stared at an empty bank account, an empty gas tank, or an empty refrigerator and wondered how to fill it back up?

Empty. That is how Peter felt the day that Jesus changed his life. His boat was empty. He expected one thing (a full boat of fish) and got another. This was devastating for a man whose profession and livelihood depended on a good catch.

> Read Luke 5:1-5. What was Peter doing when Jesus came to his boat?

How many boats were there?

1   2   3   4   5   6

How long had Peter been out fishing?

One hour   Four hours   All morning   All night

How many fish had Peter caught?

Peter was running on empty.

One of the most difficult parts of being human is to live with our hearts at peace. No matter how hard we try, relationships and situations around us spiral out of control. This leaves us feeling unbalanced and exhausted. We can start to feel restless and disappointed. Life rarely turns out the way we had once envisioned.

> What are some expectations you had for your life that have not turned out to be your reality?

One of the most difficult parts of being human is to live with our hearts at peace.

Sometimes, we can laugh at those things and say, "Thank God that never happened." For example, I was sure I would marry my high school boyfriend, which did not happen. Thankfully, God had a different and better plan, I mean *man*, for me.

Other times, we still feel a sense of loss that things turned out differently than we had hoped. A few years ago, we lost my dad to a very aggressive cancer that only gave us nine short weeks with him after we found out. I didn't think I would lose a parent that way. It was hard, painful, so sad, and completely not expected, planned for, or desired.

Read Psalm 27:13-14. What encourages you about this verse?

Emptiness comes in lots of different forms. All of it is hard. Emptiness comes from the inability to have what we expected could, should, and would be. We are not enough. Our weaknesses glare. Our flaws stare us down.

Emptiness is the emotion or feeling that is the warning light to go to God. It is our wake-up call that we need something from God. He is the only one who can fill empty things and empty people.

Where are some places that you feel empty in your life right now?

Maybe you have an empty nest at home, an empty bank account, or an empty sense of purpose in your life as you read this. Emptiness goes right to the bottom of the barrel and deeply impacts our emotions and outlook. When Jesus met Peter, He brought a fullness that Peter never expected.

Read 1 Peter 1:18-19 below. Circle the four words below that Peter wrote you were redeemed *from*. Cross out the two words Peter gives as examples of things that perish. Underline what you are redeemed *with*.

For you know that it was not with perishable things such as silver or gold that you were redeemed from the empty way of life handed down to you from your ancestors, but with the precious blood of Christ, a lamb without blemish or defect.

Once our eyes have been opened to the spiritual component of our existence, it is amazing how central it is in keeping our whole being healthy.[1] You have a soul, and it needs to be nourished. Your soul was created to connect deeply with your Creator.[2] That is why it is so easy to feel empty when we haven't been intentional in this area.[3] Our souls are often neglected since we cannot see them like we see our physical bodies.

Some signs of spiritual emptiness are listed below. Check any of the ones you are feeling right now.

☐ Lost interest in my Bible.

☐ I don't pray much or feel the need to pray.

☐ I've lost interest in church.

☐ I am more negative in my thinking about God.

☐ I don't think about my faith daily.

☐ I don't talk about my faith in regular conversations with my people.

☐ I haven't asked God for help in my hard situation.

Read Luke 5:5-6. Why did Peter let down his nets after catching nothing all night?

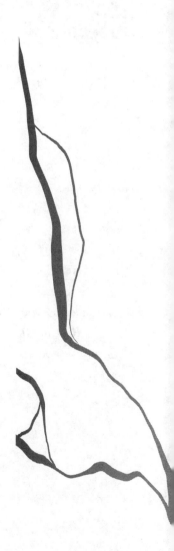

How is it different when Jesus asks us to do something we've already tried and failed?

How do you feel when you try something again after you failed at it?

How many fish did Peter catch after obeying Jesus?

Let's worship with Tauren Wells singing "Joy In The Morning."

*Though you have not seen him, you love him; and even though you do not see him now, you believe in him and are **filled** with an inexpressible and glorious joy. (1 Peter 1:8, emphasis added)*

What happened to Peter's nets?

What happened to both boats?

Abundance. Jesus brought abundance. Something out of nothing. It is something that only God can do. In one moment, Jesus brought an abundance of fish to Peter. The Spirit of God is powerful, willing, and able to bring something out of nothing.

Whatever your empty nothing is right now, do you believe Jesus can bring something out of nothing for you?

_____ Absolutely _____ Maybe _____ Probably not

When we ask God to fill us when we are empty, He reenergizes us. He brings clarity and focus. He nourishes our souls so that we have the energy to take the steps God calls us to take.

Jesus loves to surprise us in ways we don't expect. It is like an unexpected catch. We don't know where, how, or when Jesus will show up with the abundance we need. But we can be consistent in who we go to to be filled. We can be persistent in asking repeatedly.

Every answer may not be known, but we can carry on with the confidence that Jesus is working. With Jesus, there is always an unexpected catch you get to haul into the boat at some point.

WEEK 1 FOCUS VERSE: LEARN IT AND LIVE IT.

See how many blanks you can fill in today.

But you are a _____ people, a _____ priesthood, a _____ nation, God's special _____, that you may _____ the _____ of him who _____ you out of _____ into his wonderful _____ .

(1 Peter 2:9)

DAY 3: BEACON OF HOPE

I moved to California from Michigan to go to grad school. I didn't know a soul, but I did feel called. That helped. But I cried as I left, saying goodbye to my old life. Such a tangled mix of emotions—excitement about a new future but concern and worry about leaving those I knew and loved to start something new. Have you been there? Have you ever had to start something new with a mix of fear and excitement? What questions bounced around your head? *Will I be liked? Can I make it? Do I have what it takes? Will I meet new friends? Is this the right thing? Did I make a mistake? Should I go back? What does the future hold? Is God really in this? What am I doing?*

All kinds of questions dance around our minds and hearts. I wonder if this was true for Peter or if he walked with complete confidence after seeing Jesus in his boat. I imagine there was curiosity, awe, wonder, and a whole lot of excitement. What would this Jesus do next? Peter was invited to have a front-row seat with his brother Andrew, their fishing friends, and partners James and John. Mark 1:19-20 tells us that all four left their boats behind and set out with Jesus. They stepped into a new future with a new calling upon their lives and adventures to be had.

One foot in front of the other. *This is how you start.* That is how you follow someone. That is how you follow Jesus. They followed Jesus right into the town of Capernaum.

For Peter, this wasn't new. He lived in Capernaum, but he headed there with a new role, a new purpose. In some ways, that may have been even harder. Peter was not returning to Capernaum as the fisherman everyone knew. He returned home as a disciple of a new rabbi, Jesus from Nazareth.

Capernaum was one of the main trading centers in the Galilee region. It was a vibrant, active community home to about fifteen hundred people, many of whom were fishermen.[1]

> **One foot in front of the other. *This is how you start.* That is how you follow someone. That is how you follow Jesus.**

Read Matthew 4:13-17. Why did Jesus leave his hometown of Nazareth and move to Galilee?

Look up Isaiah 9:1-2, the Old Testament quote that Matthew used as his source for describing Jesus. What location would be honored?

What does Matthew 4:16 call Jesus (twice)?

Read John 8:12 and John 9:5. Write out what Jesus calls himself in these verses:

What is contrasted in these verses to what Jesus is?

How does light help us see things differently?

Light is a beacon of hope. Peter was definitely going to start seeing things differently. Following Jesus was walking with a light that shone hope, truth, love, mercy, grace, and power wherever He went. This was a big transition for Peter, a man who used to walk primarily with fishing nets. Those fishing net holes were traded for holiness that brought wholeness wherever Jesus went.

When the Sabbath day came, which for Jews was on Saturday, the community would gather in the local synagogue. Archaeological evidence shows us that synagogues were often built in the center of a Jewish community. Typically, they were built on the highest point in town or a raised platform. Synagogues allowed the Jewish community to gather regularly to be reminded of their identity and faith. The synagogue would serve as a school, meeting place, courtroom, and place of prayer for Jews.[2]

The synagogue was accessible to all adult community members, but only adult males aged thirteen or older could be elders who helped to lead. The synagogue caretaker, the hazzan, was responsible for organizing the Sabbath service and caring for the building. The hazzan would announce the coming of the Sabbath on Friday evening at sundown with blasts on a shofar (a ram's horn).[3]

On the Sabbath, the Jewish community would gather together to listen to a reading from the Old Testament Scriptures, and there would be a teaching and discussion on what it meant and how to apply it to their lives.

Read Mark 1:21-22. Where did Jesus begin His ministry in Capernaum?

These are the archaeological remains of a synagogue from approximately AD 200 that are in Capernaum. The remains include one complete wall, the ruins of the other walls, and several columns. It is white stone, unlike the characteristic black basalt rock used for other Capernaum buildings. You can still see some stucco work, frescoes, motif carvings on the walls, and Greek and Aramaic inscriptions naming the synagogue benefactors.[4]

Synagogue in Capernaum, Israel

Why were the people of Capernaum amazed when they heard Jesus teach in their synagogue?

Read Mark 1:23-28. What miracle did the people of Capernaum see Jesus perform while at the synagogue?

Describe how Jesus interacted with the impure spirit.

Look up these Scriptures. What do you notice?

- Psalm 71:22
- Isaiah 48:17
- Isaiah 54:5
- Luke 1:35
- John 6:68-69

Join Chris Tomlin and worship "Holy Forever."

According to Mark 1:28, what happened after Jesus taught in the synagogue at Capernaum?

Peter watched a demon cast out from a man he likely knew in his home village. That had to be intense. Shocking. And pretty awesome.

Read Mark 1:29-31.

We already learned at the beginning of our study that Peter had a mother-in-law, which means he was also married. We don't have any biblical accounts of his wife other than this passage about going to Peter's home and healing his mother-in-law.

What was wrong with Peter's mother-in-law and how did Jesus respond?

What did the mother-in-law do after she was healed?

Perhaps it was out of a heart overflowing with gratitude that she jumped up and got everyone something to drink, laid out a charcuterie board, and cooked up a storm.

One exciting archaeological discovery in Capernaum was a home that was slightly larger than most. Archaeologists discovered that several layers were built on top of this house. Under a fifth-century octagonal Byzantine martyrium church, excavators discovered the ruins of a simple home dating to the first century. It is what happened to the house after the middle of the first century AD that got scholars and archaeologists excited. They discovered that the house's main room was plastered over from floor to ceiling—which was unusual for houses during this time. The pottery remnants differed from the standard household cooking size. Large storage jars and oil lamps had been stored at that household.

Byzantine church built over the possible site of Peter's house.

These alterations lead scholars to believe that the home was converted to be able to hold larger gatherings of people. This is exactly how the early church began—in homes. The Byzantine church was built over the site by early fifth-century believers to help preserve and commemorate the importance of this spot in Capernaum. All of this leads historians to believe that this home was likely the house of Peter, where Jesus stayed in Capernaum. Today, you can visit this site. The Byzantine church has a glass floor, so you can see down to the first-century layer. It's pretty exciting to see where all this might have happened.[5]

Let's just recap what we've seen Jesus do in the opening chapter of Mark (which many scholars believe was Peter's account that Mark wrote down).

- Jesus miraculously brought in a huge catch of fish out of empty waters for Peter. (His profession)
- Jesus cast a demon out of a man in Peter's hometown synagogue. (His community)
- Jesus privately healed Peter's mother-in-law. (His family)

How do you think Jesus showing up for Peter in these ways was important for the relationship between Peter and Jesus?

Can you think of some ways that Jesus has shown up for you in these three areas? Has this had any long-term effect on your life or faith?

Read Mark 1:32-34.

It had been a full day already. Peter likely told his family about how he met Jesus and recounted his whole experience on the water. Maybe Peter, his brother Andrew, and friends James and John were asking questions about the demon Jesus cast out. While they enjoyed the food Peter's mother-in-law served them (perhaps alongside Peter's wife), there was a knock at the door. Someone brought a sick friend to Peter's house to see if Jesus would heal her. Then another knock, this time someone with a friend possessed by a demon. Could Jesus heal him?

What does Mark 1:33 say happened?

Archaeologists estimate that about fifteen hundred people likely lived in Capernaum during Peter's life. Those numbers may seem small today, but that was a thriving community. How many people showed up that night with people in need of healing? It's hard to say.

The Greek word πολύς (pronounced "po-lys") is used here and has the range of meaning of "many, plentiful, again and again, freely, greatly, etc."[6]

However many He healed that night, it was a lot. The people of Capernaum had a new favorite in town, and His name was Jesus.

Read Mark 1:35-39. Describe in detail what Jesus did when he got up in the morning.

What did Peter say to Jesus?

Jesus continued in a similar way to the neighboring towns with Peter and the other disciples. And so it began. Peter traveled with the Holy One of God and had a front-row view of all that Jesus wanted to reveal about God.

What is one word you would use to describe Peter's first few days with Jesus?

Jesus can do that for you too.

Write a prayer that thanks Jesus for what He is doing and ask Him to transform your weaknesses into strengths for His glory.

May He work through you so that you can be a beacon of hope for others.

WEEK 1 FOCUS VERSE: LEARN IT AND LIVE IT.

Try filling in the blanks today.

But you are a _____ people, a _____ priesthood, a _____ nation, God's special _____, that you may _____ the _____ of him who _____ you out of _____ into his wonderful _____.

(1 Peter 2:9)

DAY 4: SHINING THROUGH THE FOG

I drove back home with a surprise sitting next to me. After months of searching during the COVID-19 pandemic shortage, I finally found a puppy for our family. When I was five minutes from the house, I called my husband, and he brought out a box in our front yard so I could I sneak her inside before calling out the kids. They had no idea. When that puppy jumped out of the box, they all screamed with excitement and joy. It is a day I will never forget. That puppy has become such a special part of our family. She is always excited to see us and loves to follow me around. All the time. Everywhere. Inside and outside. From the kitchen to the bedroom. She even checks on me in the bathroom or sticks her head in the shower to make sure I'm okay and still there. I have never had such a faithful follower.

Jesus calls us to follow Him in a little different way—the way of *discipleship*.

What does being a disciple of Jesus mean? Today, we often discuss discipleship as the process of becoming more like Jesus. Where does that idea come from? Peter signed on to become one of the original disciples of Jesus, so it might help us to do a deep dive today into what discipleship looked like in the time of Jesus.

The four Gospels of Matthew, Mark, Luke, and John provide testimony of the life, death, and resurrection of Jesus. Each of these four Gospels shares similar stories but in different ways. Sometimes, this is confusing because we are reading them through the lens of our Western mindset, believing that facts should be reported chronologically with the goal of finding the correct answer. The ancient writers, however, emphasized specific stories or perspectives to

lead people through a process of discovery to help them uncover the answer. In doing this, they had a cultural narrative distinct from our Western mindsets. That can cause us to scratch our heads and wish they would speak more clearly and with fewer analogies.

We know that Matthew and John were both disciples of Jesus as part of His original twelve disciples who were His leadership team. Luke identifies himself as a physician and coworker of the apostle Paul. He authored two books of the New Testament: Luke and Acts. Acts is the book that comes directly after the four Gospel accounts of Jesus and provides the story of the coming of the Holy Spirit upon the disciples at Pentecost and the creation of the early church. Mark's Gospel is believed to have been authored by John Mark, nicknamed "Mark the Evangelist." Early church tradition from Papias of Hierapolis (c. AD 60– c. AD 130) describes John Mark as a companion and interpreter of Peter. Some scholars debate this as it is never explicitly stated in the Gospel of Mark.

> Read Luke 6:12-16 and write out the names of the twelve disciples Jesus called His apostles.

1. _____   7. _____

2. _____   8. _____

3. _____   9. _____

4. _____   10. _____

5. _____   11. _____

6. _____   12. _____

Being a disciple in the time of Jesus differed from being a student, as we would define it today. It was more like being an apprentice to learn to do things the same way. A disciple would imitate both the life and teaching of the rabbi he followed. Jesus invited these twelve men to be His disciples, to learn from Him, be changed by Him, and be fully committed to living out His teachings. A disciple in the time of Jesus would give up his entire way of life to be with his teacher. The goal was not just to listen and learn from his teacher, but also to become like his teacher to say and do what his rabbi said and did.[1]

Discipleship is at the heart of the ministry of Jesus.

Discipleship is at the heart of the ministry of Jesus. The word *disciple* is used more than 250 times in the New Testament. The New Testament was written by followers of Jesus who wanted to make more disciples of Jesus. These original twelve disciples of Jesus changed the world.

Sometimes, our churches focus on the decision to be a Christ-follower over discipleship. In Jesus's time, there was not a distinction. Disciples followed the teaching of their rabbi not because they wanted *to be* saved but because *they were* saved. It was a life of total obedience.

Peter was one of them.

Read Matthew 4:19. How did Jesus invite His disciples into a relationship with Him?

Read these passages about discipleship:

- Mark 8:34
- John 8:12
- John 10:27

What do you learn about discipleship from these verses?

Who is a teacher, mentor, or coach from whom you have learned much? What did you learn?

Jewish education was all about religious training. Learning was about history, tradition, and faith passed down through oral tradition. Early, parents and grandparents would recite the Torah (the first five books of the Old Testament) to their children. Most families did not own a copy of the Torah, so it was so important to know it by heart. The other option was to go to the local synagogue to hear the Scriptures read and discussed. Most of the education took place in three stages.[2]

STAGE ONE: BET SEFER—THE HOUSE OF THE BOOK

At the age of six, children would spend half of their day at the synagogue, learning their Hebrew letters (the first two are "alef" and "bet") and memorizing the first five books of the Old Testament (the Torah). Genesis. Exodus. Leviticus. Numbers. Deuteronomy. Memorized. The Talmud states, "Before the age of six do not accept pupils; from that age you can accept them. and stuff them with Torah like an ox."[3]

It was said that people could hear the "chirping of children" as they recited their verses. Most scholars believe both boys and girls attended the class in the synagogue. Synagogue leaders passed down the Scriptures and history of God's provision through storytelling and memorization. Parents would drop off their children at sunrise and pick them up at midday. The rest of the day would be devoted to learning the family trade of farming, fishing, carpentry, and so forth.

STAGE TWO: BET TALMUD—THE HOUSE OF LEARNING

At the age of ten, only the top students would be chosen to continue formal education. Most boys returned home to learn the family trade from their fathers, and girls returned home to learn how to care for a household from their mothers. Those who remained studied and memorized the rest of the Hebrew Scriptures (our Old Testament), except the Song of Solomon. According to the church fathers Origen (AD 185-254) and Jerome (AD 342-420), most rabbis did not allow the reading of the Song of Solomon until married or attaining thirty years of age. Students learned the Jewish art of questions and answers. Instead of responding to a question with an answer, students were taught to answer with another question to encourage curiosity and deeper study of the scriptures. Debate and discussion were highly valued. At the age of twelve, boys would become adults through a religious ceremony called a bar mitzvah.[4]

> Read Luke 2:42-47. How old was Jesus? What was he doing in the temple?

Jesus was at stage two of his education.

STAGE THREE: BET MIDRASH—THE HOUSE OF STUDY

From ages thirteen to fifteen, the best of the best would continue with their studies. The rest returned home to practice the family trade. Those who excelled in study would seek out a rabbi to study under. These students would leave their homes to devote their lives to learning from this master and become like him. This student was called a *talmid* or "disciple." Once a *talmid* chose the rabbi he wanted to sit under, he would ask if he could "follow" the rabbi. The rabbi would assess if that student had the intellectual and moral abilities as well as the commitment required to be a good disciple. The rabbi wanted to know if the boy had what it took to be like him in all areas of his life. This was considered taking on "his yoke." If the *talmid* was approved, he would hear the highly desired words "Follow me." Disciples studied by memorizing the words of their rabbi.[5]

> An ancient writing of Rabbi Yose ben Yoezer said: "Let thy house be
> a house of meeting for the Sages and sit in the very dust of their feet,
> and drink in their words with thirst."[6]

In other words, disciples were called to follow their rabbi so closely that they would get dusty from their footsteps. The *talmid* would then devote the next fifteen years of his life to that rabbi. At thirty, a *talmid* could have his own disciples and become a rabbi.[7]

Read Luke 3:23. How old was Jesus when he began His public ministry?

As Peter and the other disciples were invited to be followers of Jesus, we can see that this looked very different for them. They did not become disciples in the typical way that men in Jewish culture became disciples. Many were fishermen, but this does not mean that they were not educated. As a deeply faithful and religious community in Galilee, they knew the Hebrew Scriptures thoroughly. Yet, as with the majority of faithful Jews, they had been released into society to pursue occupations outside of religious leadership.

The disciples of Jesus were Jewish. They knew that to be called by a rabbi had deep implications for them. They had been overlooked or, at the very least, intentionally released by their culture, educational system, and synagogue structure as not having the potential to be effective religious leaders.

Jesus wandered into the Galilee region and called disciples who weren't the best of the best. They weren't the traditional disciples. They weren't the ones whom rabbis were supposed to invite.[8]

Write out the first nine words of John 15:16.

Jesus chose them. Jesus believed in them. Jesus invited them. Jesus left them with a big mission and a radical shift in who could be a disciple.

Read Matthew 28:18-20. Who does Jesus invite to be disciples?

What do you think your next step is in growing to be more like Jesus?

Take a few minutes and write a prayer in your journal or at the top of the following page asking Jesus to reveal how He wants you to grow as a disciple. What is the next step He wants you to take? How can you take action on this? Here are a few options (there are lots of others; ask Jesus what He wants for YOU):

- Attend church every Sunday
- Get baptized
- Read my Bible every day
- Memorize Scripture
- Turn to Scripture when I need to make a decision
- Pray regularly throughout the day
- Journal when I pray
- Build Christian friendships
- Listen to Jesus-honoring music
- Watch Jesus-honoring movies/content
- Tithe to my church
- Keep my language honoring God
- Keep my sexuality honoring God
- Forgive someone
- Talk about my faith with others
- Volunteer at my church, community, or a mission trip
- Let go of hatred
- Exercise self-control in this area

Let's get our worship on and proclaim our desire to follow Jesus with Chris Tomlin singing "I Will Follow."

Each step we take is like shining the way through the fog to get closer to Jesus and point others to Him.

WEEK 1 FOCUS VERSE: LEARN IT AND LIVE IT.

Fill in the blanks to your focus verse.

But you are a _____ people, a _____ priesthood, a _____ nation, God's special _____, that you may _____ the _____ of him who _____ you out of _____ into his wonderful _____ .

(1 Peter 2:9)

DAY 5: HEALING VOYAGE

In the middle of third grade, I made a dramatic decision. I decided to rock the Dorothy Hamill haircut, making the bold move of going from my lifelong hair to the bob. The boys in my class made fun of me, which was annoying and embarrassing. However, I soon discovered a cool trick. Whenever we went to one of those science museums, my hair was perfectly stacked to stand on end when I got near a plasma globe. Getting near that power source made my hair fly straight up and out. It was an invisible power that I couldn't feel but was real. It was evident to anyone around me that power was flowing through me.

As Jesus began traveling around the Galilee region, Peter and the other disciples experienced a full-blown power surge. Jesus preached, taught, and healed everywhere He went. It must have been the most exhilarating thing that Peter and the others had ever seen—the power of God in their very midst. Healings and miracles surrounded them. The laws of the universe were completely submitted to the power of Jesus. His hands healed. Bodies were restored. Lives were transformed. Roll up your sleeves and get ready; today, we enter into some sweet moments that will take your breath away.

Read Mark 5:21-24.

Mark's accounts of Jesus are action-packed. Jesus goes from one amazing moment to the next. We can hardly catch our breath from one incredible encounter to another. Jesus had just crossed the Sea of Galilee and was met by a synagogue leader.[1]

What was the name of this synagogue leader? Describe his interaction with Jesus.

By the time of Jesus, most towns had a synagogue, the center of Jewish life for the community. Synagogues were usually located in an elevated area of town to symbolize the importance of living in God's presence. Outside of each synagogue was a *mikveh*, a small pool that was used to become ceremonially clean. These are found all over Israel. The *mikveh* usually had steps down into a square or rectangular area where a person could be completely immersed in water.[2]

Ancient mikveh in Jerusalem

First-century synagogue in Gamla, Israel

Inside a synagogue, benches lined three sides of the room. Most people would sit on the floor, but important people would sit on the benches, which are called chief seats. The teacher would stand on a small platform, the *bema*. There was also a special seat called the Moses Seat, reserved for those reading from the Torah (Matthew 23:2). The scrolls and writings of the prophets were either kept in a portable chest or a permanent closet in the synagogue called the Torah closet.[3]

While Jesus and Jairus were traveling to Jairus's house, many people went with them. Jesus had His twelve disciples with Him, and a crowd formed around them. The account seems to indicate that so many people pressed in upon Jesus that it was almost mob-like. But someone managed to get through the throngs of people, desperate enough to brave the masses and push herself through them to get as near Jesus as possible.

Read Mark 5:25-34. Who got through the crowd? Why was she so determined?

What were you doing twelve years ago (yes, do the math)?
Can you imagine bleeding uncontrollably for this long?

What had she tried to do in the past to get better?

The Jewish community followed several laws about blood (Leviticus 15). This is one of the reasons that *mikvehs* were important. Whenever anyone came into contact with blood, he or she needed to go through a purification bath to be ceremonially clean, which would allow him or her to interact with God and the community again.

A woman on her menstrual cycle could not come in contact with a man while her blood was flowing—not even her husband. The same was true after she had a baby, or for anyone coming into contact with someone who had died (their blood had stopped flowing).[4] For the people of the Bible, blood meant life. For God, blood was sacred. It was life and death. God required animal sacrifices to atone for sin. Sin was so serious to God that nothing anyone could say or do would make up for it. Only the power of blood could right a wrong situation. As awful as this system seems to us today, it was very much a common part of life for the Israelites. They knew that God valued life, and this was represented in blood.

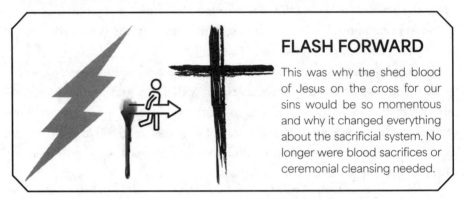

FLASH FORWARD

This was why the shed blood of Jesus on the cross for our sins would be so momentous and why it changed everything about the sacrificial system. No longer were blood sacrifices or ceremonial cleansing needed.

Since this woman in Mark 5 had a medical condition that caused her to bleed regularly, she would have been ostracized by the community for twelve years. This had to be exceedingly lonely and painful in a society that valued community and lived communally.

What did Jesus realize had gone out of Him?

Read John 13:3. What had God given Jesus?

Read Luke 8:45-46. Which disciple responds to Jesus's question?

Can you feel the tension in the air? Jesus and Jairus were already on the way to see Jairus's daughter, who was dying. They had an important job to do—a girl to save. The crowds were getting in their way, slowing them down. Then, they came to a complete stop because Jesus felt power go out of Him. They could have kept going. Jesus could have healed her and not said a word. She could have crawled back out of the crowd. But Jesus cared and wanted to talk to her.

What did the woman touch?

All she had to do was get close to Jesus. The power was so real, so strong, and so effective that she only had to get near him and touch his clothes.

Read Mark 5:32. What did Jesus keep doing?

Jesus was looking for her. He didn't want her to be overlooked. Like the parables in Luke 15 of looking for a lost sheep, lost coin, and lost son, He was willing to look for His lost daughter.

Write out what Jesus said in Mark 5:34. Circle what Jesus says healed her. Put a box around the two things that Jesus tells her to do.

Why do you think Jesus did not want her to drift back into the crowd without talking to her?

This powerful moment is interrupted by the sad news.

Read Mark 5:35-37. What was the report that came for Jairus?

How did Jesus respond to Jairus after the news came?

What do you think Jairus felt hearing Jesus's encouragement after watching Jesus heal the woman and commend her faith?

Jesus usually traveled with all twelve disciples, but on certain occasions, He took a smaller group. He may have done this to draw less attention to Himself. It may have been because the homes were small. It may have been because a group of thirteen people can be intimidating—especially in a tender moment like this household was experiencing. Whatever the reason, Jesus often took Peter, James, and John exclusively with Him for specific moments. This was one of them.

Read Mark 5:38-43. What was the scene that they arrived to at Jairus's house?

What did Jesus do?

What was the response?

> Jesus sees you right now, wherever you are, and whatever is on your heart and mind.

Whew. What a day. Jesus was never too busy to see the need or stop to talk. Jesus was intentional, kind, and compassionate. He is with you, too, dear one. Jesus sees you right now, wherever you are, and whatever is on your heart and mind.

Where do you need to pursue Jesus and just get close enough to Him that His power can restore you?

The same God who healed the women with the issue of blood for twelve years and raised Jairus's daughter from the dead is available to you. These accounts we study each day have been given to us so that we can know the compassion, kindness, and power of Jesus. It is for you, too, to embark on the healing voyage God has for you.

Write a prayer of thanksgiving that you know this same God. List all the great things that He has done.

Get your worship on today with Elevation Worship singing "Same God."

WEEK 1 FOCUS VERSE: LEARN IT AND LIVE IT.

Fill in the blanks.

But you are a _____ people, a _____ priesthood, a

_____ nation, God's special _____, that you may

_____ the _____ of him who

_____ you out of _____ into his wonderful _____ .

(1 Peter 2:9)

Video Viewer Guide: Week 1

Jesus dared to _____Peter's life.

Jesus spoke Peter's _____ language: _____ !

When there is a _____ of despair, loss, and _____,

there is only one _____.

What is His name? _____

The _____ of Jesus _____ so that _____ can spring up.

Righteousness is _____ _____ with God, self, and others.

Faith is leaning into the _____ _____ of Jesus.

Jesus allows us to _____ in our weaknesses for His _____.

The Bible's word for being perfectly flawed is _____.

Jesus brings _____ where there is _____.

The _____ of Jesus _____

so that _____ can spring up.

LEARN
with
LISA

Discussion Questions: *Week 1*

Think about these questions as you prepare to meet with your small group.

- What pet peeves do you have about others?

- What do you think about being perfectly flawed? How does that relate to how you think of yourself?

- What stands out about how Jesus connected with Peter and chose him as one of His disciples?

- Where do you need the strength of God to fill an area of weakness in your life abundantly?

- What is one thing that you would like your group to pray for you this week?

dare to care

Write down how you can encourage someone in your small group this week. When will you pray for them? When will you text them?

Hey Friend!

I was thinking of you today! How are things going? I'm praying that God will be your strength.

I can do all things through him who gives me strength. Philippians 4:13

WEEK 2

Perfectly FLAWED

and

CALLED

(Peter Walked with Jesus)

FOCUS *Verse*

*And the God of all grace, who **called you** to his eternal glory in Christ, after you have suffered a little while, will himself restore you and make you strong, firm and steadfast.*

(1 Peter 5:10, emphasis added)

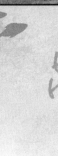

TAKE ACTION

Call up someone on the phone with whom you have not chatted in too long. Reconnect.

Serve
At a homeless shelter.

CALLED

Creation Corner

Head down to a body of water—the ocean, a lake, a river, or even a pond. As you sit by the water, reflect on how Jesus is the Living Water. How does Living Water renew our parched and weary souls? How does the majesty of the waves of the sea remind us of God's might? Read Psalm 63:1-4 and Psalm 93:4.

C R E A T E

Three words: adult coloring pages. Have you ever done one? It's relaxing and fun! Find one online, or download a free coloring page at lisatoney.com/ perfectlyflawedresources.

A Word from Peter

The Sea of Galilee was a second home to me. I knew those waters and the fish within well: tilapia, sardines, and carp. My favorite time of year was summer, when the sardines rose to the surface of the warmer waters, gorged on the plankton, and made a fat, flavorful, and abundant catch. The sea fed our families and gave us enough to trade and sell for supplies. Just down the way a bit was the Jordan River, which flowed right into our sea. Combined with the underground springs, the waters were always fresh, cool, and inviting. We often jumped off the boat on a hot day to cool off, and the countless early mornings before dawn shaped me. It was hard work but honest work.

לָדוּג | da•gim, dag | fish

Did you know there is only one Hebrew word for fish? I know you call every fish by a different name, but we just called them fish. We ate a lot of fish. It was one of the foods in Israel that was plentiful, nutritious, and permitted by God.

Whether big or small, fish are *dagim* (*dag* is a single fish).

I'm unsure how it happened, but I apparently got a fish named after me. If you visit Israel one day, you will likely be invited to dine on "St. Peter's fish." Today, you call it tilapia. It's a delicious and plentiful fish in the Sea of Galilee. I recommend it.

One thing I loved about Jesus is that He used plain, ordinary things to help us better understand how God saw us and what God wanted for our lives. Jesus used fish as a teaching illustration lots of times. He even performed miracles with them. Those moments were powerful not only because I was a fisherman but also because I think of Jesus and what He taught us every time I saw or ate a fish.

Perhaps most remarkably, when Jesus invited me to follow Him, He asked me to use my skills in a new way. I didn't really understand it at first. Jesus asked me to fish for people. That seemed crazy. Most of the time, I felt like a fish out of water. But I just kept my eyes on Jesus as I followed Him one step at a time. Fishing with Jesus is not what I did; it became my whole reason for being.

Shalom,

Simon Peter

DAY 1: NETTING INSIGHT

On any given night, I love to read to my kids. There is something about reading a good story out loud that draws us all in. Words can create beautiful, profound, and memorable pictures for us. Stories woven around characters, adventures, and powerful themes inspire us and give us opportunities to think differently.

Jesus also loved stories and taught using them. These were called parables because they were stories told to teach something. The brilliance of using stories to teach is that stories are easier to remember. Once Jesus told the story, the disciples could retell it and so could those listening to it.

Read Matthew 13:34-35. What did Jesus use to teach His followers?

Read Psalm 78:1-4. This is the verse that Jesus referenced. What does Psalm 78:4 emphasize?

Read Matthew 13:10-17. What did Peter and the other disciples ask Jesus?

Stories make things easier to remember. They stick with us because we connect with the people in the story. Often, we can retell the story to someone else. This was a genius teaching strategy in a culture dependent upon oral tradition. It is a great way to make complex ideas easier to convey and understand.

In our Western mindset, however, we sometimes overemphasize answers. We look for the right answer or the correct information.

Jesus often changed the trajectory of many questions by telling a story. He seemed to ignore the questions to talk about something totally different. He was not negating their questions but seeking to teach them in a way they would remember. Most of His parables did not come with explanations. They were meant to inspire people to think about, examine, and apply the lessons. Parables were rich with meaning, instruction, and inspiration.

What did Jesus say was given to the disciples in Matthew 13:11?

Jesus contrasted people who do not believe from those who have faith. Write out Matthew 13:16.

Why do you think some people have ears to hear and eyes to see and others do not?

In the first-century culture, a parable was a story that highlighted a relatable human experience and was used to explain a spiritual reality. Language cannot convey the breadth and depth of God's greatness, wisdom, and authority, so Jesus used physical imagery through stories and metaphors to teach theological insights into how God does things. He often used these stories to contrast how people lived and how God was inviting them to live.[1]

As believers today, we are invited to step into a better story. When people could relate to the characters in the story, Jesus connected deep truths about God's shocking grace, relentless love, powerful healing, exquisite forgiveness, surprising justice, and deep loathing of even a hint of evil. When one had ears to hear and eyes to see, it was impossible not to want to be in a relationship with a God who excelled beyond anything around them with goodness, truth, and justice.

Let's read one of Jesus's parables, in which Peter specifically speaks up to ask Jesus about it.

Read Luke 12:35-40. What would you name this parable?

The emphasis or theme of this parable can be found by reading the first line as Jesus began this parable. Look at Luke 12:35. What did Jesus say we should be ready for?

Who did Jesus encourage us to be like? (Hint: Luke 12:36)

What were the servants holding? (Hint: Luke 12:35)

Light is a powerful metaphor in Scripture and for our faith. Light punches holes in the darkness and provides a whole new way to see things.

Read John 8:12. What did Jesus call Himself?

What did the servants need to be ready to do and how fast? (Hint: Luke 12:36)

Who do you think are the servants and master in this story?

What do you notice as a condition for the servant listed in Luke 12:35 and Luke 12:37?

My love for fashion gets me very distracted in these verses. I start thinking about what I should be wearing and when I can go shopping. Can I get an "Amen" from any fashionistas out there?

As much as Jesus appreciates creativity, His point here is not about what we should wear physically. Remember, parables always point to spiritual truths. So whenever we read a parable, we must focus on this question: what spiritual truth is Jesus trying to teach me?[2]

> **Parables always point to spiritual truths.**

In Luke 12:38, 43, how did Jesus describe the situation for the servants if they were equipped, prepared, and actively ready to serve?

Plot twist. Something unexpected happens.

Instead of the servant being the one who served the master, what happened to the servant who was faithful to the master and was ready to take action in His midst? (Hint: Luke 12:37)

Jesus calls us into active service as we wait for His return. He commends waiting. "Waiting for God to act is my favorite…" said no one. Ever. I don't know about you, but I'm chronically impatient. When I need God to act, I need Him now. God seems to be in the habit of making us wait. Why is it so important to God that we learn patience?

Waiting on God is one of the hardest challenges of being a faithful follower of Jesus. In our insta-world of insta-everything, waiting seems lame. We rush ahead, move forward, create our own destiny, or so the world tells us to do.

Are you in a season of waiting on the Lord? Describe it below.

> **Waiting on God is one of the hardest challenges of being a faithful follower of Jesus.**

Write out Psalm 38:15 in the margin. Circle the word *wait*. Underline the *word* answer.

Peter noticed a shift in the discussion in Luke 12:38-40. He asked Jesus about it in Luke 12:41. I can envision Peter nodding along in agreement at the beginning of Jesus's story. "I'm with you, Jesus. I'm tracking." Then he tilts his head and scratches his hair. Hm…wait…who are we talking about? Is this about me and the disciples or about other people?"

Jesus didn't give him an answer. Rather, he continued with additional plot twists in the parable.

If Jesus had ended his parable before verse 40, we could focus on the main point being faithfulness, but Jesus began to throw in other scenarios of what servants might do.

Read Luke 12:42-48.

What if the servant decided that his master would be gone for a long time, so he neglected his responsibility; lived it up, wining and dining; and even treated those he managed abusively? The assumption was that the master would never know what the servant did while he was gone, so he could do whatever he wanted.

Jesus threw in a twist: what we do when no one is looking is important. God sees. God knows. Our character is not just about what we do when others have eyes on us, but who we are all the time. We see the repercussions for those who were servants of the master who squandered their responsibility. There were different levels of punishment based on what the servants did.

1. The servant who was blatantly and knowingly disobedient, doing the opposite of what was asked by the master, had very harsh repercussions. In fact, Jesus pointed out in Matthew 10:33 that He would deny before God anyone who rejected Him.
2. The servant who knew what the master wanted but failed to do it faced some harsh discipline—consequences that must be lived with.
3. The servant who failed to obey the master, because he did not know what or how to obey, was disciplined with a lighter hand.[3]

Write out the last sentence of Luke 12:48.

What do you think that Jesus has entrusted you with?

Get your worship on today with Elevation Worship singing "Jesus, I Come."

Write a prayer based on this parable that Peter and the other disciples learned from Jesus. What does it stir up in you? What did God speak to your heart as we were working through this parable together? Where are you netting your own insight from Jesus? What kind of servant do you want to be?

WEEK 2 FOCUS VERSE: LEARN IT AND LIVE IT.

Try filling in the blanks to help you learn the verse. You can look back if you need some help. Practice each day, and pretty soon you will have it. The Holy Spirit will activate it in your head and heart right when you need to hear from God most.

And the _____ of all _____, who _____ _____ to his eternal _____ in _____ , after you have _____ a little _____, will himself _____ you and make you _____, _____ and _____.

(1 Peter 5:10)

DAY 2: THE CREW'S QUEST

When I started college, I was excited and nervous to meet my roommate, with whom I would share a dorm room. We took the basic compatibility test and got matched by the school. Thankfully, my roommate, Ann, was wonderful, and we got along really well.

For colleges to use a test to pair students off as roommates, when they are setting off on the adventure of adulting for the first time away from their families, is quite genius. It means having an instant buddy—doing things in a pair is always better. There's someone to talk to, learn from, laugh with, and build community. It is a natural way to alleviate stress.

Thankfully, Jesus had a group of friends with whom He spent time. They were His disciples. He taught, mentored, and challenged them. He modeled for them and equipped them to continue His work after He left them. Let's look today at how Jesus shepherded this motley crew.

Read Matthew 9:35-38. Where did Jesus go on his journeys?

What did Jesus do and say in each place?

How did Jesus feel about the people He met?

What animal did Jesus compare people to?

An article reported by the Associated Press covered a story out of Istanbul, Turkey, about sheep that went over a cliff. Their shepherds were having breakfast and left them alone. Sheep do not have a good sense of direction, and when part of a herd walked off a cliff, the rest really did follow them over the edge. The sheep in the back couldn't see past the sheep in front, so they didn't know what was happening ahead. The first 450 died, and the remaining 1,050 in the flock were saved from the cushioned fall that the first 450 provided.[1] Isn't that crazy?

Read Isaiah 53:6. What does the prophet Isaiah compare us to?

Sheep in the Middle East were plentiful and valuable. They provided wool, milk, meat, and skins to make parchment. They also were used for sacrifices

Let's get our worship on with Patrick Mayberry singing "Lead On Good Shepherd."

in the temple. Sheep could easily adapt to the climate in the Middle East, but they need a shepherd more than any other animal does. Here are some fun facts about sheep:

- Sheep easily go astray. If one gets lost, it has no homing system to return home. It wanders around until the shepherd finds it and returns it to the flock.
- Sheep are defenseless. They have no natural ability to fend off predators. They huddle together in a flock and walk in circles, hoping they are not the ones that will get eaten.
- Sheep spend most of their day eating, but they'll eat anything they see, even poisonous weeds. They need a shepherd to lead them to green pastures to eat safely.
- Sheep have a flocking instinct. When they get separated from their flock, their anxiety level rises. A lost sheep will walk around in circles, bleating in distress. When its shepherd finds it and brings it back to the flock, it calms down again, secure, content, and happy.
- When ewes are pregnant or a sheep's wool gets wet and heavy, they easily fall over and get trapped on their backs. They cannot right themselves, and if their shepherd does not intervene, their internal gases will build, and they will suffocate and die.[2]

Do you ever feel like a sheep? How?

Read John 10:11 and John 10:14-15. What did Jesus call Himself?

Jesus is our Good Shepherd who leads us.

Jesus cares for His sheep. He sees them. He knows them. He protects them. He goes after the one that cannot right itself. He is our Good Shepherd who leads us.

What a beautiful proclamation that we need and want Jesus to lead us in all we do. We know Jesus had a plan and purpose to gather a leadership team. Let's dive in and see the "why" behind what Jesus was doing as He prepared His team to go out.

Write out what Jesus said to Peter and the other disciples in Matthew 9:37-38.

What an encouragement. The harvest is ripe. That means there are so many opportunities to share the good news of Jesus with others. The people are ready; we just need willing workers.

Stop and ask God to send out more workers to proclaim the good news of the kingdom of heaven and heal those afflicted. Who is working to reap the harvest? Take a few minutes today to write an encouragement email, text, or letter to send to someone doing this work.

Have you ever felt a calling in your own life to be in ministry?

All of us are called to be ready to share with others. Missionaries and pastors are not the only ones who get in on the joy of the harvest.

But in your hearts revere Christ as Lord. Always be prepared to give an answer to everyone who asks you to give the reason for the hope that you have. But do this with gentleness and respect.

(1 Peter 3:15)

Jesus was training, teaching, and giving the disciples the opportunity to begin this great work. It was not just about listening to Jesus but putting what one heard into practice.

Read Matthew 10:1-8. Jesus sent Peter and the other disciples out to do just as they had watched Him do. No longer were they witnesses but participants in the ministry.[3] What did Jesus give His disciples the authority to do when he sent them out on their missionary journey? Circle all that apply:

Heal the sick	Make friends	Take no extra bag
Recruit more disciples	Sing loudly for all to hear	Bless homes with peace

Preach	Raise the dead	Take no staff
Earn money	Sell lemonade	Take no shoes
Cast out demons	Run for office	Take no photos
Heal lepers	Take no money	Stay in homes
Heal every disease	Take no extra clothes	Freely give

Where and to whom did Jesus tell the disciples not to go on their missionary journey in Matthew 10:5?

1.

2.

Read Matthew 15:24. Who does it say that Jesus was sent to?

Read Matthew 10:16. How did Jesus describe the disciples as He was sending them out?

I don't know about you, but I would be scared out of my mind. That sounds like I was being sent out to be eaten alive.

Jesus gave the disciples three animals as examples to imitate. What are they?

1.

2.

3.

What animal did Jesus say they were being sent out among?

Read Matthew 10:17-42.

Whew. These are some *intense* words. After reading this training that Jesus gave His disciples, look again at the three animals he encouraged them to imitate.

What qualities from each animal do you think the disciples needed on this missionary journey?

In this passage, how often did Jesus tell them not to be afraid?

Let's make a list of all the ways Jesus was trying to prepare them to be bold and courageous despite persecution, doubt, and disbelief. I'll give you the verse cue, and you write out how Jesus equipped, empowered, and encouraged His leadership team.

Write the promise or words from Matthew 10 that instructed them on how to respond or how God would provide for them.

(v. 19) _____

(v. 20) _____

(v. 22) _____

(v. 23) _____

(v. 25) _____

(v. 28) _____

(v. 29) _____

(v. 30) _____

(v. 31) _____

(v. 32) _____

(v. 39) _____

(v. 40) _____

(v. 41) _____

Do you remember when we read Matthew 10:5 and wrote down two groups that Jesus specifically told the disciples to avoid? The Gentiles (anyone not Jewish) and the Samaritans (half-Jewish and half-Gentile—both ethnically and religiously). Jesus had a strategic plan to reach all people at the right time and way.

Look at this gem in Matthew 10:18. Who does Jesus tell the disciples they will get to go before and share the teachings of Jesus, even though their focus is specifically on the Jews?

And I tell you that you are Peter, and on this rock I will build my church, and the gates of Hades will not overcome it.
(Matthew 16:18)

Peter and the disciples were chosen to be part of a big, messy, complicated, dangerous mission that would change the world. They could not do this in their own strength, only the power of God. Jesus laid out all the obstacles, trials, and persecutions they would face. All the evils of humanity and the enemy would be thrown at them, but God's power would overcome them. They would not be able to do this hard thing on their own strength. In fact, it was likely impossible. Only by the power of God, which Jesus generously equipped them with, could these common, ordinary men do impossible things to begin to build the kingdom of heaven here on earth. This crew's quest was all about Jesus.

WEEK 2 FOCUS VERSE: LEARN IT AND LIVE IT.

Try filling in the blanks today.

And the _____ of all _____ , who _____ _____ to his eternal _____ in _____ , after you have _____ a little _____ , will himself _____ you and make you _____ , _____ and _____ .

(1 Peter 5:10)

DAY 3: SEAS OF PLENTY

I love a good fish story. This is a giant fish that I caught a few summers ago when I was visiting my parents in Michigan. This fish was so heavy, my arms hurt. It was fun because I posted a picture on social media of me with

My Fish Story

my fish, and guys from my high school suddenly came out of the woodwork asking if I caught that in our lake and how I caught it. I kept them guessing for a while before the truth came out...

The real story is that I caught it by picking it up—because it was floating in the water when I went for a walk on the beach. I carried it home to show my dad. I thought he'd get a kick out of it, and then my fish story grew... as they do.

Fish were a staple source of protein during the time of Jesus. Especially in the Galilee region, fish were abundant because of the fresh water in the Sea of Galilee. Local fishermen today talk of a few main types of fish: sardines, bing (carp-like), catfish, and *musht* (tilapia). Tilapia is so popular today it is served in restaurants around the Sea of Galilee as "St. Peter's fish." Tilapia quickly mature and reproduce and are easy to catch because they stay close to the water's surface. They swim close together and can be caught easily with nets.[1]

In Jesus's day, Jewish people did not eat catfish because they were considered unclean. Catfish do not have fins and scales and don't qualify as edible fish according to the Levitical code that Jews followed (Leviticus 11:19). Peter and other fishermen could still sell them on the eastern side of the Sea of Galilee to the Greek communities that did eat them.[2]

Peter knew a lot about fish, and when Jesus called him to be a disciple, He told Peter that He would teach him how to fish for people instead.

A fish was one of the early symbols that Christians began using as a covert way to identify themselves to one another. The first reference to this is from Clement of Alexandria, born in AD 150. In addition, archaeological discoveries provide historical evidence of the fish being an early cave tattoo.[3]

Then Jesus said to Simon, "Don't be afraid; **from now on you will fish for people.***"* *(Luke 5:10, emphasis added)*

Ichthus drawn on a cave wall

A Christ-follower during times of persecution could draw one half of the fish in the dirt, and unless the other knew the response, it just looked like they were doodling. But if another Christ-follower knew the response, they would put a second mark to complete the fish. A fish could also be put on a cave wall to indicate where Christians gathered.

Sometimes, the Greek letters for an acronym representing the saying, "Jesus Christ God's Son is Savior," would be included inside the fish symbol. These letters became known as *ichthys* or *ichthus* from the Greek ἰχθύς, pronounced ikhthūs, or "ICK-THOOS," and means fish.

I–Iota or Iesous (which means Jesus)
X–Chi or Christos (which means Christ)
N–Theta or Theou (which means God)
Y–Upsilon or Yidos/Huios (which means Son)
Y–Sigma or Soter (which means Savior).

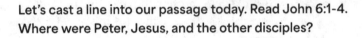

Let's cast a line into our passage today. Read John 6:1-4.
Where were Peter, Jesus, and the other disciples?

Why was a great crowd following Jesus?

Where did Jesus go with the crowd?

Which Jewish festival was near?

Passover was one of the festivals that God required the Hebrew nation to celebrate. It was a huge festival where people would go to Jerusalem, and they would remember the great Exodus out of Egypt. The Hebrews had been enslaved by Egypt for 430 years, and God sent to them a leader named Moses to lead them out of exile into a new promised land that would become their new home.

Since people were gathering for Passover, crowds were traveling. This is why such large numbers could gather to hear Jesus, this new rabbi, teach. His unique message held their attention. They loved it so much they stayed to listen. And stayed. And stayed. As Jesus taught, it got late, and the disciples began to become concerned about handling the needs of all these people. That was a lot of mouths to feed.

Read John 6:5-7. Who did Jesus talk to about getting bread for the crowd and how much did the person say it would cost to feed this crowd?

Read John 6:8-9. Which disciple came forward with some food? What was it? Who offered it?

Read John 6:10-11. What did Jesus have the people do? What did Jesus do with the bread and fish?

Jesus gave thanks to His Father before performing this miracle. Why do you think these two things were connected?

How does this connection between thanksgiving and miracles impact how you talk with God when you need His strength in your weakness?

How much food was given to each person in the crowd?

Read John 6:12-13. What did Jesus tell Peter and the other disciples to do?

Worship time. Let's sing "King Jesus" with Brooke Ligertwood.

*Grace and peace to you from him who is, and who was, and who is to come, and from the seven spirits before his throne, and from Jesus Christ, who is the faithful witness, the firstborn from the dead, and **the ruler of the kings of the earth**. (Revelation 1:4-5, emphasis added)*

How much was collected?

The number twelve is often represented in Scripture as a symbol of the completeness of God's governing authority. There were twelve tribes of Israel in the Old Testament and twelve disciples whom Jesus asked to be part of His leadership team.[4]

Read John 6:14-15. What was the people's response?

What did Jesus know that the people wanted to do with Him?

To avoid this, where did Jesus go?

Why do you think that Jesus did not want to be king in the way that the people expected and hoped He would?

Jesus was King, but not in the traditional sense. The people only knew kings as political leaders. Israel was so tired of being captured by other people groups. Their history was littered with captors (Babylonians, Assyrians, Romans, etc.) that overcame this small nation.[5] They were ready for a mighty political leader who would free them and protect them from the ongoing turmoil of captivity once and for all.

Jesus miraculously fed people on this day. Not only is He able to do big things but He is also able to provide for our small everyday needs.

There are seven foods listed in Scripture that Israel celebrates as native to the land.

1. Wheat
2. Barley
3. Figs
4. Pomegranates
5. Grapes
6. Olives
7. Dates
(Date honey)

These thrived in the hot desert sun and provided abundant food for the people of this land. Jesus often used them as teaching illustrations to help people better understand who He was.

Read John 6:25-29.

The crowd wanted more of Jesus. They got in their boats and followed Him to Capernaum. Finding Jesus, the people wanted to know more about Him. Jesus began to challenge the people to think more deeply. He had miraculously fed the crowd; with amazement, they wanted to see more of what He could do. In turn, Jesus began teaching about what was needed deep in their souls. Bread for bodies, yes, but there was more to human existence than being satisfied by food. A person also needed soul food.

How did Jesus describe to the crowd what they need?

Read John 6:35. What did Jesus call Himself? What do you think Jesus meant by this?

You likely eat three meals a day. If you skip a meal, your tummy rumbles and you feel discomfort. Your body needs food. You wouldn't have lunch one day and then decide you were good to not each lunch until next week. Your body would respond loudly that it needs food. Jesus was talking about being the bread we need for life.

How do you nourish your soul regularly? What rhythms do you have, or what rhythms would you like to create to find that nourishment?

For the LORD your God is bringing you into a good land—a land with brooks, streams, and deep springs gushing out into the valleys and hills; a land with wheat and barley, vines and fig trees, pomegranates, olive oil and honey; a land where bread will not be scarce and you will lack nothing. (Deuteronomy 8:7-9)

> **When you are a follower of Jesus, you get adopted into God's family—a special _royal_ family. That makes you a daughter of the King.**

As King of kings and Lord of lords, Jesus is the ultimate King over all royalty, nations, and tribes. When you are a follower of Jesus, you get adopted into God's family—a special _royal_ family. That makes you a daughter of the King.

Write a prayer to King Jesus expressing how this makes you feel.

WEEK 2 FOCUS VERSE: LEARN IT AND LIVE IT.

Try filling in the blanks to help you learn the verse.

And the _____ of all _____, who _____ _____ to his

eternal _____ in _____ , after you have _____ a

little _____ , will himself _____ you and make you

_____ , _____ and _____ .

(1 Peter 5:10)

DAY 4: COURSE CORRECTION

I think I spend half of my life as a mom reminding my kids to wash their hands before they eat, brush their teeth twice a day, take a bath before bed, and keep their hands away from their mouths. They don't seem to believe that germs are real. Those invisible microscopic guys sneak in when least expected—usually before a big event where everyone needs to be healthy.

Everyone has a different level of germ tolerance. I was once traveling through an airport and saw a single dad traveling with two young children. He was holding their hands and stuff and had just gotten them some food. Of course, one of the kids promptly dropped their food on the airport floor. Dad picked it up, brushed it off, and handed it right back to him. I cringed. Airport floors seem particularly nasty, with a few kazillion shoes on them every second. But then I also sympathized. The guy had just spent a million dollars on a slice of airport pizza. Did he really have the time and energy to stand back in line and do it all again while they were trying to get to the gate?

I blessed him in Jesus's name and prayed the airport cooties off that piece of pizza for that sweet boy as I rushed to my gate. We serve a big God.

God gave the Israelites several ceremonial cleansing instructions in the Old Testament. These served a few purposes: sanitary guidance, comfort, health, and the ability to model lessons about being clean on the outside *and* on the inside.

Today, we are going to look at an encounter that Peter, the other disciples, and Jesus had with the Pharisees (the religious leaders of the day).

Read Matthew 15:1-10. Where did the Pharisees travel from to see Jesus and accuse the disciples of breaking God's Law?

What were the disciples doing that made the Pharisees ask this?

As we read this, we may be thinking the Pharisees are right. The disciples should be washing their hands before they eat. That is gross. I hear you.

Don't worry; cleanliness was also a value in the ancient world. The heat and dust created a dynamic duo that begged for frequent washing for both health and refreshment. It was customary for a host to provide travelers with a basin of water to clean their hands and feet to prepare for a meal after a journey.

Read Genesis 18:4; 19:2; 1 Samuel 25:41; and John 13:1-10. What do these passages all have in common?

Ancient Roman Washbasin

Priests were also required to wash their hands and feet before providing their services (Exodus 30:18-21). Eventually, the Pharisees took these special ceremonial purity instructions and applied them across the board to all Israelites.[1]

The problem was that the Pharisees were adding to God's commands something that God had not asked. They had given themselves a divine authority that Jesus was trying to untangle. The Pharisees's teaching was getting passed down from generation to generation and becoming a tradition that was accepted equally with Scripture.

As the Pharisees asked Jesus a question, Jesus responded, as a good rabbi does, with another question. Jesus focused on one of the Ten Commandments that taught the Israelites to honor their father and mother. Jesus then accused the Pharisees of being hypocrites and quoted a prophet from the Old Testament named Isaiah.

Read Isaiah 29:13. What does this passage say about two different ways to worship God?

Jesus quoted this passage to illustrate the difference between what the Pharisees were doing and what God wanted. The Pharisees did not focus on worshipping and exalting God; rather, they were more about correcting, teaching, and being rule-givers to the people of Israel. They focused more on oral law tradition than the Scriptures. The oral law was known as *paradosis* or the "tradition of the elders."[2]

Jesus called out the Pharisees for playing God by making up laws that God had not given them. There is only one God, and it was not them.

And…it is not us.

The ideas and things that we pass down as part of our family traditions need always to be viewed through this lens. Do we hold our traditions, rules, and customs as more important than the instructions of God? Our job as followers of Jesus (disciples) is to discern when we need to make changes in our lives and families when we have gotten off course.

What are some of the traditions that your family keeps (holidays, family gatherings, stories, sayings, vacations, and so forth)? List them at the top of the following page. Then look at them through the lens of honoring God.

- Put a star by the ones you know are in line with God.
- Put a question mark next to those about which you are not sure.
- Draw a line through the one you know are not honoring God or supporting the teachings of Scripture.

Now, what will you do with these? The choice is yours. You can always create new traditions.

After Jesus confronted the Pharisees, Jesus called the crowds to Him and continued to teach.

Write out what Jesus said in Matthew 15:11.

Jesus set up a strong contrast between the teachings of the Pharisees and Himself. Pharisees were expected to teach the people how to follow the laws of God. Jesus gave an alternative teaching about cleanliness and told the Pharisees publicly that they were against God. Uh-oh. Insulting the religious leaders of the day might get a little...complicated.

Jesus had just positioned Himself as a critic of the day's powerful political and religious leaders. He blatantly called their teaching heretical and undermined their authority and influence with the people. The disciples were a little uneasy.[3]

Read Matthew 15:12. What did the disciples think Jesus had done?

They may not have understood everything Jesus did or said, but they knew enough to feel the tension in the air and know that Jesus was messing with the big dogs. It did not bode well for them or Jesus.

But Jesus knew what He was doing. The time had come for Jesus to begin to separate Himself from the other religious leaders of the day. He was not just another teacher, He was the *one* they had been waiting for. He was the one and only Son of God. His teaching was above all others.

Again, Jesus, being a good rabbi, answered their question with a story that didn't directly answer their question but would require deeper thought and perhaps even multiple meanings.

Read Matthew 15:13-14.

Jesus started talking about plants and blind guides. Can you see the disciples looking at Jesus trying to track with Him, trying to connect the dots, trying to make sense of it all? They were scratching their heads and looking at one another, hoping someone had figured it out. Peter finally gave up and just asked.

Read Matthew 15:15. What did Peter ask Jesus for?

I'm with Peter here. This one has some layers that are hard to understand when you first hear it. Let's break it down to see if we can see what Jesus was doing here.

Jesus first said that the Pharisees were like plants that God did not plant. The teachings of oral tradition, because they were not from God, would be pulled out (by their roots) from the authority and influence they had with the people. Then Jesus compared the Pharisees to the blind. Not only were they blind to their own spiritual reality, but they were blindly leading the people away from God's will (and would fall in a pit).[4]

Read Matthew 15:16-20. How did Jesus describe the disciples?

The Greek word here for dull is ἀσύνετος or *asynetos*. The range of meaning includes "foolish" or "without understanding."[5]

Jesus brought back the teaching to the main point the Pharisees had brought up. Jesus, the Son of God, the promised Messiah, was here to teach them about the deeper things of the soul. He wasn't saying that hand washing didn't matter, but rather that a clean soul was way more important than clean hands.

In Matthew 15:18, where did Jesus say our words come from?

In Matthew 15:19, what things did Jesus list as evil thoughts that reside in the human heart?

1.

2.

3.

4.

5.

This was not an exhaustive list, but rather a strong list of examples.

Take a minute and check your own heart on each of these things. Have any of these things flickered in your heart and words?

Jesus is far more worried about the evil we face and fight daily than He is about handwashing. He wants hands that are clean from doing wrong and hearts that are pure from the effects of evil and sin.

Jesus revealed how our spiritual hearts harbor many bad thoughts and ideas. Our hearts, minds, and souls need Jesus to cleanse them and bring a righteousness that only He can bring. *Righteousness* is a word that the Bible uses to talk about healthy relationships—a right relationship with God and right relationships with others.

> Our hearts, minds, and souls need Jesus to cleanse them and bring a righteousness that only He can bring.

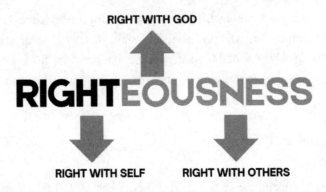

RIGHT WITH GOD

RIGHTEOUSNESS

RIGHT WITH SELF   **RIGHT WITH OTHERS**

Let's get your worship on. Enjoy "Good Grace" by Hillsong United.

The time had finally come. God sent Jesus, and that was joyous, glorious, great news. Jesus came with the mission to usher in the kingdom of God, a kingdom filled with goodness, kindness, gentleness, peace, patience, love, joy, faithfulness, and self-control (Galatians 5:22). Jesus wants to fill our lives with these good things rather than letting the bad stuff rule the day.

Jesus was all about inside-out disciples. He wanted to begin with the inside rather than the outside—and He still does today. How is your heart?

WEEK 2 FOCUS VERSE: LEARN IT AND LIVE IT.

Fill in the blanks to help you learn your verse.

And the _____ of all _____, who _____ _____ to his eternal _____ in _____ , after you have _____ a little _____, will himself _____ you and make you _____ , _____ and _____ .

(1 Peter 5:10)

DAY 5: CHARTING COMPASSION

As a kid, I went on a camping trip with my parents and siblings. One of the stops we made was at a waterfall. My older sister skipped ahead of me and ran her hand along a wooden handrail. All of a sudden, she shrieked in pain and had a hand full of splinters. I'm not sure which was worse, her having to sit and have my mom and dad pull them all out of her hand or me cringing and watching. Every. Single. One.

That memory is emblazoned upon my soul whenever I think about forgiveness because whenever we wound one another, it is like a sharp shard is driven into our souls. We can't see wounds as we can see splinters, but oh, can we feel them.

Every lie, betrayal, abuse, neglect, slander, and awful things that are said or done can pile up inside. Splinters poking everywhere. They can make us cynical and bitter. Hurt people hurt people, and we end up causing pain because we are in pain. It's a vicious cycle, isn't it?

The Bible calls all this evil and wrongdoing *sin*. I used to hate that word. But I've come to be thankful for it because we need a word that can speak to the horrible, grievous acts that evil causes. Not only do I need that word for the sin that lurks in my dark heart but also for all that has been inflicted upon me. I did not want it, ask for it, or deserve it. You too, my friend, you too. Many hard, dark things out there wound us deeply. Sometimes it feels like too much.

For this, we have Jesus. Say it with me. For **this**, we have Jesus.

We need someone so powerful and soul-capable to get in there and remove those splinters just like my sister's hand. We need Jesus, the Son of God Almighty, the Bright Morning Star, the Sun of Righteousness, the Resurrection, and the Truth and the Life…who also happens to be a carpenter. He knows how to handle the wood shards embedded in our souls.

Today, we will read a teaching that Jesus gave Peter and the other disciples about forgiveness. Jesus lays out a plan for how we are to handle when people wrong us.

Read Matthew 18:15-17. List out the four steps.

1.

2.

3.

4.

Jesus laid out a plan for us to know what to do when someone wrongs us.

1. Talk to the person and tell them what they did and how you feel about it. The hope is they will receive this, apologize, you can forgive them, and move on in the relationship.
2. If this doesn't happen, the next step is to take one or two other people with you to talk to the person so that there is more accountability with another perspective. The hope is that the others involved can help bring peace to the situation.

Hurt people hurt people, and we end up causing pain because we are in pain. It's a vicious cycle.

3. If this doesn't happen, the next step is to talk to a pastor at your church to ask for help intervening in this situation. The hope is that a spiritual leader will be able to usher in a new level of peace and restoration.

4. If this doesn't happen, then Jesus says you have tried all you can do and are free from any further obligation to try to reconcile.

Have you ever had the opportunity to go through these steps with someone? How did it go?

It's crazy hard, isn't it? Our hearts are fragile, and our emotions can collide with reason easily, making it complicated. Sometimes, it feels easier to stay mad. Sometimes, it feels easier to do nothing. Sometimes, it feels easier to get revenge.

But, for *this*, we have Jesus. We have Jesus to help us do hard things. We have Jesus to help us be strong when we feel weak. Jesus transforms our weaknesses into strengths.

Read Matthew 18:18. What do you think this verse means?

Read Matthew 18:19-20.

These verses are often discussed when we are praying together. After this teaching, Peter approached Jesus with a question about forgiveness.

Read Matthew 18:21. What was Peter's question?

Peter had a number in mind. How many times did Peter think he should forgive someone?

_____ 1	_____ 3	_____ 5	_____ 7	_____ 9	_____ 11
_____ 2	_____ 4	_____ 6	_____ 8	_____ 10	_____ 12

Peter did not just pull this number out of the air. Judaism taught that three times was enough to show a forgiving spirit.[1]

> **We have Jesus to help us do hard things. We have Jesus to help us be strong when we feel weak. Jesus transforms our weaknesses into strengths.**

Peter was taking the traditional number of their faith and doubling it. He even added one for good measure. Seven was viewed as the number of completeness. So Peter's dialogue with Jesus was actually very thoughtful and showed Peter growing in his faith. He was trying to think with the abundance that he had seen Jesus displaying around him.[2]

The restoration of a relationship in a family, friendship, work environment, school, or church is complex because each person involved has an extended network of relationships to consider. Peter was wrestling with the discipleship path—one we still try to walk today—that prepares a heart to be ready to forgive and restore anyone who repents. However, wisdom dictates that discernment is needed to know if the person who repents is sincere or is speaking empty words, only to return to the same sinful behavior pattern. Chronic repeaters can cause a lot of damage. Relationships and lives can be deeply impacted and hurt through repeated sin. Peter may have been thinking about this as he asked about the limits of forgiveness.[3]

Read Matthew 18:22.

Jesus also had a number in mind. How many times did Jesus say we should forgive someone?

_____ 15 _____ 24 _____ 32 _____ 44 _____ 50 _____ 77

Jesus gave a number. Does that mean we can start a tally? Stop forgiving when we hit 78? Keeping count is exhausting! Jesus was making a point by multiplying Peter's number. There is no limit to how much we could forgive.

At heart, Jesus was communicating to Peter and the other disciples the need to seek out reconciliation.[4] We should be wise, and when possible, forgive and restore relationships. It may not always be possible. But if someone repents and we forgive them, we should look for ways to move forward in the healthiest way possible with that relationship. It takes time, it takes building trust again, and it won't go back to how it was before, but it can have a new beginning.

Jesus then told a parable about forgiveness.

Read Matthew 18:23-35.

How did the king treat his servant who owed him a debt?

How did the king's servant treat *his* servant?

What happened when the king learned how his servant treated *his* servant?

Jesus used this parable to point out the huge debt we can never repay with the piles of sins we have collected. Jesus talked about the consequences of this sin—and was setting the stage for the incredible gift He was about to give every person as He went to the cross. He died for our sins so that we can receive God's forgiveness as a free gift of grace. Nothing we can do can earn it. It is a gift.

For the wages of sin is death, but the gift of God is eternal life in Christ Jesus our Lord. (Romans 6:23)

How does Matthew 18:35 impact the way that you prioritize and practice forgiveness?

Jesus's teaching on forgiveness is so challenging, radical even. It is this strong because He wants to align hardened human hearts with the heart of a God who is willing to forgive each of us so much. God must expose the ways we have wronged Him so that we can see the path He wants us to walk regarding forgiveness and reconciliation with others.

Read Jeremiah 31:34; Hebrews 8:12. What is so amazing about these verses?

Write out Ephesians 4:31-32.

Draw a heart and put a splinter in it for each hurt you have where you have been wronged or hurt by another. Write the name of the hurt or person beside each one.

Let's spend some time in worship by singing "Holy Water" by We The Kingdom.

Spend some time praying over them, asking God to help you know how to remove the anger, hurt, and pain so that you can take the steps necessary to forgive. If you are in a place where you can do it, get a bandage and stick it on top of the heart as you ask Jesus to bind up your brokenness and move you toward wholeness. He can help you chart a course of compassion.

WEEK 2 FOCUS VERSE: LEARN IT AND LIVE IT.

Try filling in the blanks to help you learn the verse.

And the _____ of all _____, who _____ _____ to his

eternal _____ in _____ , after you have _____ a

little _____, will himself _____ you and make you

_____, _____ and _____.

(1 Peter 5:10)

Video Viewer Guide: *Week 2*

When Jesus is _____, we can let go of _____.

Peter was willing to _____ _____ of the boat to _____ _____ to Jesus.

Courage means _____ _____.

Fear _____ , and courage _____.

When you move _____ Jesus, He _____ you.

Ditch the _____ and clear your _____.

We are called to take action _____ Jesus.

LEARN with LISA

Discussion Questions: *Week 2*

Think about these questions as you prepare to meet with your small group.

- **What is something hard that you have done?**

- **What is something that you are afraid of?**

- **What stands out about the account of Peter walking on the water?**

- **Where do you need to keep your focus on Jesus this week?**

- **What is one thing that you would like your group to pray for you this week?**

invest in people

Write down how you can encourage someone in your small group this week. When will you pray for them? When will you text them?

Hey Friend!

Want to get together for a coffee date?

I'd love to hear how things are going in your life.

God is our refuge and strength, an ever-present help in trouble. Psalm 46:1

Perfectly
FLAWED
and
HOPEFUL

(Peter Learned from Jesus)

FOCUS *Verse*

Praise be to the God and Father of our Lord Jesus Christ! In his great mercy he has given us new birth into a living hope through the resurrection of Jesus Christ from the dead.

(1 Peter 1:3)

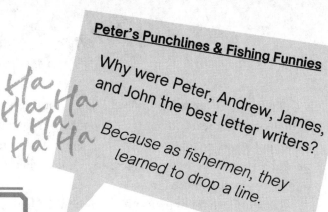

Ha Ha Ha Ha Ha

TAKE ACTION

What feels like a hopeless issue in the news right now? Take one step to bring hope to the situation.

Serve

At a seniors center.

HOPEFUL

Creation Corner

Find a place where you can sit among rocks or climb them. Rocks are solid and strong like our God. As you feel their hefty weight and sturdy placement, consider how God gives us a sure foundation in which to live.
Read Psalm 18:2.

CREATE

What season is it? Make a wreath for your front door to welcome others and offer them HOPE.

A Word from Peter

My boat was my second home. I spent countless hours in it. My father, brother, and I had so many good times with our friends James and John, who also owned boats. Ours was made of wood, but it was not big or fancy. The men in our family had fished for generations. It was what we did and who we were. Imagine my shock when a wandering itinerant rabbi came by and wanted to get into my boat.

After a bad night of no fish, I was not in the best mood. But there was just something about Jesus that caused me to listen to Him. Best decision I ever made. He changed everything for me. I never thought I would do anything else but fish. Jesus got me out of my boat and onto dry land to follow Him—which I did for the rest of my life. He told me I'd still fish—but for people instead of swimmers. After the haul of fish He put in my boat that morning, I believed He could do anything.

We actually got to spend some time on boats. Jesus walked out to us once in the middle of a storm that popped up while we were trying to cross the Sea of Galilee. We were all exhausted and thought we were seeing things. We thought He was a ghost. It was Jesus, *walking* on the water. That guy. He always knew how to shock us. I even got out of my boat to make sure it was really Him and got to walk on water too. But as soon as I took my eyes off Jesus, I started to sink. I was terrified. I was between the boat and Jesus, and I thought one of them should be able to save me. And I was right, but it wasn't my boat. It was Jesus.

I used to feel at home in my boat, but home became wherever Jesus was. That was pretty crazy for a fisherman like me.

Shalom,

Simon Peter

DAY 1: NETTING WONDERS

Have you ever played the game Simon Says with a group of kids? It is a great exercise to learn how to follow the leader. But the game gets tricky because the leader can easily lead players astray if they aren't paying close attention. Fast and furious motions can sometimes become the group's focus, and it is easy to forget to listen to the instructions and follow the guiding principle of the game—only move when Simon says to.

As far as we know, this game was not named for Simon Peter, but it could have been. Peter was a leader in the making. Sometimes, he got it right. Sometimes, he got it wrong. But he kept leaning in. Peter stayed the course even when Jesus exposed his weaknesses. Peter was learning in painful, embarrassing ways that our flaws leave us far from perfect. Yet, in Jesus's presence, flaws can be reformed when we remain faithful. Reshaped. Reworked. Jesus used Peter's flaws to help shape him into a new kind of man—a new kind of leader.

What is one of your flaws that you would like to change?

How have you asked Jesus to help reshape your flaw?

We've looked at the list of disciples before, but let's look more closely at one of the lists that Scripture gives us.

Read Matthew 10:2-4. Make a list of the twelve disciples.

1.

2.

3.

4.

5.

6.

7.

8.

9.

10.

11.

12.

Yet you, LORD, are our Father.
   We are the clay, you are the potter; we are all the work of your hand.
       (Isaiah 64:8)

In Greek, the word *first* is πρῶτος, which is pronounced "prōtos." It is often used to designate the one listed first in an order of importance or to designate a leader.[1]

Matthew emphasized Peter's role as the leader of the disciples. This is why Peter was highlighted among the disciples so often. Jesus spent extra time preparing Peter for the role he would play with the disciples and later in leading the establishment of the early church after Jesus was crucified, resurrected, and ascended back to the right hand of God in heaven.[2]

Early on, not long after they first met, Jesus said that Simon would be called Peter (John 1:42). However, in the Gospel of Matthew, when Jesus speaks to Simon, He calls him Simon until the exchange we will read about today.

Jesus led the disciples out of the Galilee region to a very different kind of place—Caesarea Philippi. This beautiful area was located in the basin of Mount Hermon. As the snow melted from the peak of Mount Hermon, it seeped into the ground, and a cold but clear stream led to the Jordan River flowing from the mouth of a large cave found in Caesarea Philippi.

Caesarea Philippi was located about twenty-five miles from the Jewish communities in the Galilee region, but it was a very different environment. It was an area that was notorious for pagan activity.

This area was a center of Baal worship in Old Testament times. Baal was the Canaanite-Phoenician god of fertility and weather. The Bible often mentions "high places" built for pagan gods. People would find the higher ground of hills and build altars to their gods, believing it would get them closer to the deities.[3]

Illustration of the Greek god Pan

Later, the Greeks used this location to worship the Greek god Pan, who was the god of shepherds, hunters, and the untamed wilderness. Archaeologists have discovered, in a large open cave where the water flows, niches that held statues of Pan, a half-man and half-goat who played the panpipe. The large cave in Caesarea Philippi was considered a gateway to the underworld of Hades or hell, where the fertility gods lived during the winter and returned to Earth each spring. Each spring, the people of Caesarea Philippi engaged in wicked deeds, including prostitution and sexual depravity, to entice the return of Pan. A statue of Pan would even be paraded around during festivals.[4]

When the Romans conquered the area, Herod the Great constructed a temple of white marble to honor Caesar. Eighteen years later, Herod's son Philip inherited the site and named it Caesarea. Since there was also a Caesarea along the Mediterranean Sea where Herod's palace stood, he added his name to it to distinguish the location, calling it Caesarea Philippi. Even after the Romans had conquered the area, people continued to worship Pan. Today, this area is known as Banias because Arabic has no letter for *p*. The location morphed from Panias (for Pan) to Banias.[5]

It was to this "redlight district" of their day that Jesus brought Peter and the disciples.

Read Matthew 16:13-20. What did Jesus ask the disciples?

What were the four answers that they gave Jesus?

1.

2.

3.

4.

Jesus must have turned and looked directly at Peter because the word *you* used in Matthew 16:15 is singular, not plural.[6] Jesus was not asking all the disciples, but rather Peter specifically.

What did Peter say in Matthew 16:16?

Whew, baby. Full stop. This is a BIG DEAL. The Messiah was the promised One whom all of Israel, God's chosen people, had awaited. They had prayed for it. They had hoped for it. They had dreamed of it. They had watched and waited. The Messiah was to be the One that God sent to save His people. And now…Jesus said the moment had come. The Messiah was He.

Read a few of these verses about the promised Messiah:

- Jeremiah 23:5
- Isaiah 11:1-16
- Zechariah 9:9
- Isaiah 7:14
- Micah 5:2
- Isaiah 53:1-12
- Deuteronomy 18:18-19
- Daniel 7:13-14

What stands out to you about them?

In this place of idols and wickedness, Peter named Jesus the Messiah, and Jesus said, "Yes, I am."

In Matthew 16:17, who did Jesus say revealed this to Peter?

In the margin, write out Matthew 16:18. Circle what Jesus is going to build His church upon. Underline how strong it will be. Highlight who is going to build the church.

It is helpful to note that *Jesus* was going to build His church, and He pointed to Peter as the one whom Jesus would use to establish this movement. Peter would be the foundation,[7] but Jesus would use all His team in these efforts— and He continues to build His church today…as He will in the future.

Jesus brought His team to this pagan place full of sin and immorality and said, "I am going to change all this. All of *you* are going to change this. There is a different way to live, a better way to live. Even when the culture is dark and evil, I am stronger than all of this. I am strong when you are weak."

Jesus blessed, equipped, and empowered them with His strength to do hard things. What a beautiful hope and vision for the future as they stood in a very dark place.

What did Jesus order the disciples not to do in Matthew 16:20?

Why was this important?

Timing was important to Jesus. He showed Himself strong often by the power of restraint. Revealing His identity to the disciples was important because they were heading to Jerusalem, where the atmosphere would become increasingly hostile toward Jesus. Jesus trusted His disciples with this powerful truth.

Read Matthew 16:21. What did Jesus reveal after this wonderful, awe-filled moment?

Jesus began to prepare the disciples for the journey to Jerusalem and the events that would unfold while they were there. This was the first time they heard that they were heading into a death trap for Jesus. He would be killed. I often wonder if they missed the "on the third day be raised to life" because they were so overwhelmed with shock and grief that Jesus was going to die and leave them.

Read Matthew 16:22. Where did Peter take Jesus? What did Peter say?

The word for *rebuke* in Greek is ἐπιτιμάω and is pronounced "epitimaō." It means to rebuke or to warn.[8]

Why do you think Peter disagreed with what Jesus said so strongly?

It took determination for Jesus to stay true to the mission that God had called Him to complete. Peter's idea to rescue Him must have sounded very tempting. The disciples did not know what we know now. All they knew was that their rabbi, teacher, friend, and Messiah was going to die.

Read Matthew 16:23 to see how Jesus responded to Peter's reaction. What did Jesus say to Peter in response?

Can you feel the electricity in the air? The tension? Emotions heightened. Disbelief. Doubt. Fear. Anxiety. Anger. Peter pushed back on Jesus, and Jesus pushed back on Peter.

The same leader Jesus said would be the foundation of His church was now called Satan. Don't worry; Jesus wasn't saying that Peter *actually* was Satan.

The Greek word used here is Σατανᾶς which is pronounced "Satanas." It means adversary, opponent, or Satan. Jesus was likely calling Peter an opponent or adversary to God's will for Jesus.[9]

Read Matthew 16:24-28. What does Jesus call us to do if we want to be His disciples? What do you think this means for your life here and now?

Jesus did not give up on Peter in the midst of a heated exchange. This faith journey was shaping Peter's character, perseverance, and passion to be the rock to build the church.

Write a prayer to Jesus about being your firm foundation and your commitment to stand strong even amid a culture that pushes back against living a life of faith in Jesus.

WEEK 3 FOCUS VERSE: LEARN IT AND LIVE IT.

Try filling in the blanks to help you learn the verse.

Praise be to the _____ and _____ of our Lord _____

_____! In his great _____ he has given us new _____

into a living _____ through the _____ of

_____ _____ from the dead.

(1 Peter 1:3)

DAY 2: SUNRISE

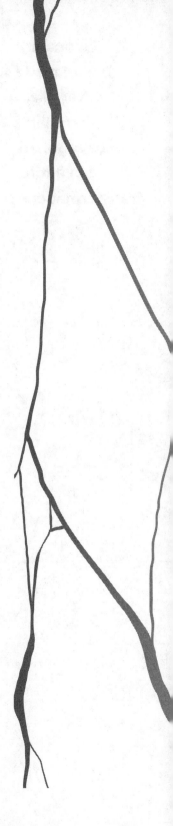

When I moved to California to go to seminary, my native Californian roommate told me her mom always said the palm trees were God's paint brushes He used to create the earth and then stuck in the ground. I've always loved that idea.

I hope to be part of the sunset painting posse when I get to heaven. It never ceases to take my breath away to see the splendor of color that God paints across the sky every sunrise and sunset. It is amazing. Every. Single. Time.

Jesus was exactly this remarkable to the disciples. Just when they thought they knew who this surprising Jesus was, He would do something they never dreamed of. You ready? Buckle in; today is SO GOOD.

Read Matthew 17:1-3. How many days after their time in Caesarea Philippi did Jesus go up to a high mountain?

_____ 4　　　_____ 3　　　_____ 7　　　_____ 6

Who did Jesus take with Him?

_____ Peter, James, and Thomas　　　_____ Peter and Andrew

_____ Peter, James, and John　　　_____ All the disciples

Read Luke 9:28. Why did Jesus take them up the mountain?

Usually, after climbing a steep mountain, everyone wants to see the vista. Once the climbers have huffed and puffed up a mountainside, they are rewarded with a different perspective. The disciples with Jesus got to see something spectacular for sure, but it was definitely not what they were expecting.

What happened to Jesus when they reached the mountaintop in Matthew 17:2?

The Greek word used here is μεταμορφόω, which is pronounced "metamorphoō." Guess what word we get from this Greek word?

**I wonder if
God made
caterpillars
to remind
us regularly
of beautiful
transformations.**

If you guessed *metamorphosis*, you are right. It means "to be changed in form." I wonder if God made caterpillars to remind us regularly of beautiful transformations.

What did Jesus's face and clothes look like in Matthew 17:2?

Later, John would write something very profound. Write out John 1:14. Circle what John says we would see.

God revealed the splendor and glory of Jesus to the three disciples on that mountaintop. Who appeared with Jesus on the mountaintop?

1.

2.

These two men were major figures in the Old Testament. God used both men in mighty ways. God used Moses to lead the Israelites out of slavery in the land of Egypt from Pharaoh. Elijah was a prophet who called Israel to repent from worship of the false god Baal and return to God.

Both men also met God on a mountaintop during their lifetimes. Moses met God on top of Mount Sinai and received the Ten Commandments. Elijah met God on top of Mount Horeb to stand in the presence of the Lord. A mighty wind, earthquake, and fire all passed by Elijah, but the Lord was not in any of them. Only after all those events did the Lord's presence come in a gentle whisper.[1]

For these two mighty men of the past to appear with Jesus revealed that there was life after death. It also declared the greatness of Jesus, who transcended both in His majesty. Jesus was elevated above the revered Moses and Elijah because He alone was the Son of God.

Peter, James, and John must have been frozen in their sandals, wide-eyed, with jaws dropped.

Read Matthew 17:4. What did Peter offer to do in this holy, majestic moment when two dead patriarchs of the faith appeared, and Jesus started glowing on the mountain?

As one would. Oh, Peter.

No one knew what to make of Peter's offer. Maybe Peter wanted these guys to stick around for a while so they could hang out. It's not every day that you can ask Moses about the burning bush, parting the Red Sea, or going up against Pharaoh.

Read Matthew 17:5. What appeared in the sky while Peter was still speaking?

There was even more glowing. Jesus's face looked like the sun. His clothes were radiating light, and a bright cloud moved over all of them, going from bright to even brighter.

What did the voice from heaven say?

Read Matthew 3:16-17. What did the voice from heaven say when Jesus was baptized at the beginning of His ministry?

In both events, who did God declare Jesus to be?

Read John 3:16. What did God call Jesus?

At the Transfiguration, God gave the directive to listen to all that Jesus said. It was a megaphone from heaven, complete with a bright spotlight. Unforgettable. Talk about an experience that gets seared into a guy's memory.

Peter would also reflect on this moment later. Read 2 Peter 1:16-19. What did Peter want to rise in the people's hearts in verse 19?

What did John call Jesus in Revelation 22:16?

Where do you think some of this imagery may have come from?

The "bright morning star" is a star that outshines all the others. Peter, James, and John all witnessed this during the Transfiguration.

Read Matthew 17:6-8. What did the disciples do?

What did Jesus do and say?

Can you think of another time Jesus told Peter not to be afraid?

Worship with Zach Williams and Dolly Parton in "There Was Jesus."

When they looked up from that terrifying moment, Jesus was there. He alone was their focus. Moses and Elijah had faded away, and there was Jesus.

Read Matthew 17:9. What did Jesus tell the disciples to do with what they had just witnessed?

Silence was necessary so that Jesus could reveal things according to His timing. The Jewish nation wanted a political messiah to overthrow the rule of Rome. But Jesus had not come as a political savior for Israel but to be the Savior of this world from sin.[2]

As they walked down the mountain, the disciples wrestled with what they saw and what it meant, as well as aligned it with some of the Scriptures they knew about Elijah.

Read Matthew 17:9-13. Who did the disciples ask Jesus about?

Read the Old Testament prophecy in Malachi 4:5-6, then read the New Testament description of John the Baptist in Luke 1:17. What do you notice?

Both of these men had a special mission: to prepare the way for Jesus to come. They had done their job so that Jesus could do His.

The Transfiguration is especially powerful when we look at it in light of the transformation that God can do in us. The same Greek word used for "transfiguration" in this account is later used by Paul to talk about God's power in our lives. Do you remember our Greek word μεταμορφόω (metamorphoō)?

Look up these two passages and choose one to write out:

- Romans 12:2
- 2 Corinthians 3:18

Where do you need transformation in your life?

In what way does someone you love need transformation in their life?

In what way does our world need the power of God's transformation?

Draw a sun that shines brightly to remind you of the power of the SON of God to bring powerful transformation.

WEEK 3 FOCUS VERSE: LEARN IT AND LIVE IT.

Try filling in the blanks to help you learn the verse.

Praise be to the _____ and _____ of our Lord _____

_____! In his great _____ he has given us new _____

into a living _____ through the _____ of

_____ _____ from the dead.

(1 Peter 1:3)

DAY 3: MARITIME MONEY

One of my first jobs was as a waitress at a little family restaurant called The Pine Pantry. All of the wait staff had to start as dishwashers and then work their way up to becoming servers. My older sister worked there, so it was a lot of fun when I graduated from doing dishes to being a waitress with her. She taught me the ropes, and we would tag team to cover the entire restaurant together. Eventually, my younger sister worked there too. It was a sisters' thing. Would you like your eggs OE, SCR, or SUNNY UP? I can write food abbreviations with the best of them.

On payday, I was always excited to see the money I had earned after spending so many hours smelling like french fries. *But wait, what was this?* I didn't get all the money I earned. Some was removed for this mysterious invisible monster that gobbled some of my income: taxes.

What was your first job when you had taxes taken out of your paycheck?

Don't get me wrong; taxes do a lot of good things. They build roads, libraries, parks, and schools. I appreciate being part of a system that utilizes taxes for the common good. It is hard to keep that in mind when all you see is money deducted on payday!

Taxes. You can't escape them. Even back in the time of Jesus, taxes existed.

Rome was in control of the territory of the land of Israel. Still, they let the Israelite community have a lot of freedom in utilizing their language, religion, cultures, foods, and traditions. But they did have to pay taxes. Some taxes had to be paid to Rome, and there were also taxes to be paid at the temple.[1]

Coins of at least three different nations were used in everyday life in Judea during the time of Jesus. Greek coins, Roman coins, and Jewish coins were all in circulation. This may feel very confusing to us, but the people of the day were used to it. They used different coins to pay different groups, and money changers were available to make exchanges.

The high priest was responsible for collecting the temple tax. There would be highly visible containers shaped like trumpets in the community where people would place their temple tax. In some areas, temple representatives of the Jerusalem priesthood would walk throughout the territories collecting the temple tax.[2]

Read Matthew 17:24-27. Where were Jesus and the disciples?

Do you remember whose hometown this was? (Hint: Matthew 4:18)

Who came and talked with Peter in Matthew 17:24? What was his concern?

How did Peter answer?

_____ Yes   _____ That's ridiculous   _____ How do you spend it?

_____ No   _____ Not in this lifetime   _____ God is above taxes

The Old Testament (Exodus 30:11-16) called for everyone over twenty years of age to pay a half-shekel to support the Tabernacle (this was a predecessor to the current temple). This same financial support transferred to the temple when it was built.

The Jewish half-shekel was the equivalent of the Greek silver *didrachma*, a "two-drachma piece" coin. This tax was paid by the Israelites and went toward the upkeep of the temple. Priests serving at the temple were exempt from the tax.[3]

Which disciple was a tax collector? (Hint: Matthew 9:9)

Example of a didrachma coin. Courtesy of Wikimedia Commons.

The Gospel of Matthew is the only one of the four Gospels (Matthew, Mark, Luke, and John) to report this account. Matthew, a tax collector, must have found this particular teaching pretty interesting.

The temple tax collectors were not the same as Matthew, though. Matthew collected taxes for Rome. Perhaps the tax collector approached Peter because he was the leader of the group. This account may have been an attempt to trap Jesus, but Peter assured the collector that Jesus paid His taxes just like everyone else.[4]

Read Mark 12:13-17. What did Jesus say about paying taxes to Rome?

Jesus likely overheard Peter's exchange with the tax collector and saw this as a good teaching moment. Jesus talked about duty and taxes. He asked Peter if a government leader (a king) taxed his children or others. Peter replied that a king charged others, not his own family members.

Write out what Jesus said in response to Peter in Matthew 17:26.

This one statement says some profound things. Let's explore things a bit more.

Read Luke 2:41-50. Where did Jesus tell His parents that He had been?

Read Psalm 27:4. What is the temple called?

Jesus emphasized to Peter that He is God's Son. God is Jesus's father and the ultimate King of all. As a family member, Jesus would not need to pay the temple tax because the temple was God's house of worship. Jesus also extended this identity of the family of God to Peter and all those who followed Jesus.[5]

Read Matthew 12:48-50. Who did Jesus say was His family?

> **God is Jesus's father and the ultimate King of all.**

There would no longer be a need a sacrifice to the temple because Jesus was about to become that ultimate sacrifice for all people for all time.

Read Hebrews 7:26-27. These verses talk about Jesus as our High Priest. He met the role of high priest so that we no longer need one in the temple making sacrifices for our sins. What words did the writer use to describe Jesus?

Jesus, and by extension His disciples, did not *need* to pay the temple tax in light of these truths. But, out of an abundance of concern for those who had not discovered this, Jesus told Peter that they should pay the tax.[6]

Jesus highlighted the importance of not offending the government. Jesus, using self-control, restrained His rights as the Son of God for the good of others. He was always committed to doing things according to God's will and timing. Jesus agreed to pay the temple tax so that the offense He might have caused would not hinder people from coming to Him. Paul later used the same idea that Jesus had taught Peter to instruct the early church.

Read Romans 4:13-23.

What does the Spirit bring to mind as you read these verses?

Can you think of an example of how you might apply this idea in your life with someone you know?

Taxes must be paid, but Jesus had a little fun with it. Go, Jesus. Way to make paying taxes fun—and memorable for Peter. Peter got to go fishing. That was his love language after all.

Jesus told Peter to throw out a fishing line to catch a fish so he would find the money for paying the tax. Peter was used to using big nets to fish. But Jesus wasn't asking Peter to return to doing what he used to do; rather, He used something from Peter's past for a new purpose.

One fish. That was all Peter needed. It was like a treasure hunt on the open sea.

Peter must have laughed so hard. Remember how Jesus first caught Peter's attention with a boatload of fish? Now, Jesus was holding Peter's attention with just one fish. The first fish that Peter caught would be enough. It would hold the provision that they needed to pay the temple tax. Jesus had provided a fish with a coin in its mouth.

What are some skills or experiences from your past that you haven't used in a while? It's fun to think that God may not be done with them yet. He may have a way to repurpose them yet.

The fish known in Israel today as "St. Peter's fish" is tilapia. There is no way to know if that is the same type of fish that Peter caught that day. Whenever I take groups to the Holy Land on a tour, we have some fun with this. We'll eat at a restaurant, and people can order a fillet or whole St. Peter's fish with the heads still on. I always challenge our groups to kiss their fish; maybe they'll find a coin in its mouth, just like Peter did.

The coin Peter found that day was a four-drachma coin or one shekel—enough to pay the taxes for Peter and Jesus.[7] The coin in the fish's mouth was another miraculous indicator of Jesus as the Son of God. The temple had stood for a long time, reminding the people to hope for God's promised salvation. Now that salvation had arrived.

Kissing St. Peter's fish (2023)

This story helps us understand the importance of paying taxes. But what about when the government asks us to do something against what Jesus asks of us? That is when things get complicated.

Can you think of some things your government has asked of you that are contrary to what Jesus asks of His followers?

We belong to Jesus first, above our loyalty to government. We must run all things through that filter. Here are a few questions to ask about any political conflict you may face.

- Jesus, how do you want me to respond?
- Jesus, what can you show me in your Word to help me think about this?
- Holy Spirit, how can you embolden me to represent Christ in this situation?
- How can I be light in the darkness?
- Where can God transform my weaknesses into strengths for His glory?

Write a prayer asking the Lord to lead your thinking, guard your heart, and help you be slow to anger, filled with words of kindness and impact.

WEEK 3 FOCUS VERSE: LEARN IT AND LIVE IT.

Try filling in the blanks to help you learn the verse.

Praise be to the _____ and _____ of our Lord _____ _____! In his great _____ he has given us new _____ into a living _____ through the _____ of _____ _____ from the dead.

(1 Peter 1:3)

DAY 4: TREASURE TROVE

Who are the friends you turn to when life is hard? Friends who love you through mixed-up emotions, mood swings, tears, loss of words, and lots of words. I texted one of my dearest friends when I got the phone call that my dad had died, and she didn't even text back; she just got in her car and came to my house. She sat with me while I cried. I treasure that moment.

Friends like that are important for all of us—even Jesus. Jesus and the disciples began their journey to Jerusalem, where Jesus would soon be crucified. Mark 11 reports that for three days, Jesus and the disciples entered Jerusalem and then left to stay in Bethany at night. We don't know for sure, but perhaps they were staying with Jesus's dear friends Mary, Martha, and Lazarus, who lived in Bethany. As the emotional pressure and political tensions began to increase around Jesus, I can only imagine that staying at a friend's home would help ease some of the burden and stress. Sitting around a table with a good meal and friends is always good for the soul.

The first day that Jesus entered Jerusalem was joyful.

Read Mark 11:1-11.
Who did Jesus send
to get a donkey?
Where did Jesus ride the donkey?

Jesus entered Jerusalem among the cheers of the people, on a humble donkey rather than a stallion that would befit a military commander.

Why do you think Jesus so humbly entered into Jerusalem?

In a world where everyone is seeking fame and notoriety, how do you think humility can set a Christ-follower apart from the things of this world?

Look up these verses about humility.

- Proverbs 11:2
- Philippians 2:3
- Colossians 3:12
- James 3:13
- 1 Peter 5:5

Write out which one speaks most strongly to you today. What impacts you about it?

Perfectly Flawed—And Hopeful **101**

After Peter, Jesus, and the disciples entered Jerusalem, where did they go? (Hint: Mark 11:11) Why did they leave?

This was the end of the first day of the three-day trek back and forth to Bethany that Jesus made. On day two, Jesus and the disciples began their walk back to Bethany. The road would still have been littered with the palm fronds from the parade the day before. People had cut and waved their palm fronds to honor and celebrate Jesus as their King.

Read Mark 11:12-14. What did Jesus and the disciples walk past?

What did Jesus say to the tree?

What did Mark say about the tree?

We have this strange encounter with the fig tree. Mark wrote that it was not the season for figs. Jesus knew that. There was something else going on here beyond the fig tree not having fruit. Just when we hope that Jesus would tell us more or explain it to the disciples, Mark left his readers hanging with an interruption in that story. But he would come back to it.

Jesus wasn't mad at a fig tree because it had only leaves and no fruit. The tree was not in season to bear fruit. He used it as a visual illustration. Jesus was about to walk into the temple, which *should* be in season, bearing spiritual fruit for God, but He would not see fruit.

Jesus walked back by that same tree again a few verses later, and it was withered, dead, and destroyed, symbolic of what would happen to the temple. We'll get back to the fig tree tomorrow, but first, let's check out what this interruption was all about.

Mark reports that Peter, Jesus, and the other disciples walked into the temple when they arrived in Jerusalem.

Read Mark 11:15-16. What did Jesus see happening in the temple courts?

Jesus was in the outermost courtyard where both Jews and Gentiles gathered. It was an entrepreneur's dream to set up a shop to make it more convenient for the Jews who needed to have animals to atone for their sins. Sacrificed animals seem awful to us, but it was a cultural norm for them. God had placed a high value on blood throughout the Law because life was in the blood. Jesus would soon pour out His own blood on the cross, giving His life for all of us so that this messy, smelly, bloody, costly system of animal sacrifice could change. Jesus would become the final, perfect, and complete sacrifice for our sins.

How did Jesus react when He reached the courtyard?

What in the world was going on with Jesus? Was he having a really bad day? Was this grumpy Jesus? Hangry Jesus? Why would the one we know to be full of compassion, healing, mercy, and love get so riled up? Talking to trees and flipping tables…Did he just lose it one day?

Thankfully, Jesus sat at far more tables than he flipped. But not this time. Today was a different kind of teaching moment. Jesus aligned himself with the prophets of old who used to behave outlandishly to get people's attention so they could hear a message from God when they, like us, got too caught up in their own greed and selfish pleasures to pay attention to what God was calling them to do. The Old Testament prophets would sound the alarm bells to call people back to a God-honoring lifestyle.

Jesus's actions were like that alarm bell. Jesus walked purposefully into the temple courts. The temple was overwhelmingly huge and majestic. It was like combining twenty-five to thirty football stadiums together in the center of Jerusalem. This was the center of Hebrew life; the center of the Jewish faith. It was busy, full of people, animals, and noise. Coins flashed and clanked; doves flew about, and sheep jumped around. Feather, fur, and wool mixed with chirping and bleating. Jesus looked around at the temple meant for people to encounter God Almighty and saw it had become a business center. Where was the sound of worship? Where were the people of prayer? Where were the hearts of repentance? Where was the focus on the Father? It broke His heart.

Like a parent who, out of an abundance of emotional care, sees a child about to touch a hot stove and yells STOP, Jesus looked at the people He had come to save and saw them distracted by the things of this earth. There was an appearance of prayer and being busy for the things of God, but Jesus saw no prayer, no worship, and no focus on the heart of God. Jesus, filled with strong emotion, started flipping tables over to warn them to flip their hearts and focus back on God.

If you really care about someone, don't you warn when you see something concerning and breaking your heart? Jesus was doing that same thing here.

Jesus also made a profound prophetic statement. The massive temple so central to Jerusalem and Jewish life was going to be destroyed.

Don't you know that you yourselves are God's temple and that God's Spirit dwells in your midst? (1 Corinthians 3:16)

Read 1 Corinthians 3:16 in the margin. Circle who is God's temple. Underline who dwells in our midst.

Everything was about to change. God's people, not a building, would become the new temple.

Jesus was crucified somewhere around AD 30, and the destruction of Jerusalem was not far behind. Forty years later, in AD 70, Rome decimated Jerusalem and destroyed the temple.

I wonder if, in those horrific sounds of war, in the midst of the destruction of Jerusalem and the temple, the echo of tables being flipped by a surprising Jewish rabbi rang in anyone's ears or memories.

The Western Wall

After the destruction of the temple, only one retaining wall remained—we know it today as the Western Wall or the Wailing Wall. Ironically enough, today, it *is* dedicated to prayer. It is a place where people worldwide come to PRAY. People even write their prayers and leave them in the wall.

Read Mark 11:17. What was Jesus doing?

When Jesus walked into those temple courts and flipped those tables, He taught with every word and every action—flipping tables to flip the focus back onto what mattered.

What did Jesus say His house should be?

*But Christ is faithful as the Son over God's house. And **we are his house**, if indeed we hold firmly to our confidence and the hope in which we glory.*
(Hebrews 3:6, emphasis added)

*For through him we both have access to the Father by one Spirit. Consequently, you are no longer foreigners and strangers, but fellow citizens with God's people and also **members of his household**, built on the foundation of the apostles and prophets, with Christ Jesus himself as the chief cornerstone.*
(Ephesians 2:18-20, emphasis added)

Who would God's House be for? (Hint: Mark 11:17)

*And they sang a new song, saying: "You are worthy to take the scroll and to open its seals, because you were slain, and with your blood you purchased for God **persons from every tribe and language and people and nation**."*
(Revelation 5:9, emphasis added)

What was it instead of a house of prayer? (Hint: Mark 11:17)

Jesus quoted from prophets (Isaiah 56:7; Jeremiah 7:11) who were very familiar to the Jewish community. These prophets contrasted the behavior of the people with God's commands. They spoke of love, joy, and covenant faithfulness in the temple. Instead of goodness, the prayers of the people had been corrupted by deceptive words, false gods, theft, injustice, adultery, and oppression of the poor.[1] The people would show up at the temple thinking they could look good on the outside and fool God about their everyday choices. But Jesus said, "Remember." God is no one's fool. God's house will not be given over to the enemy that robs, deceives, and steals the joy of the Lord.

Robbed. Robbed by the enemy.

Getting robbed means someone takes something from you. Have you ever been robbed (Amazon packages, credit cards, bank accounts hacked, identity stolen, and so forth)? Write about it below:

Anger is like an iceberg. You only see the top part, but underneath, there are many more emotions.

I've even had my tomato cages stolen out of my garden. *Who does that?*

How did you feel when you were robbed?

It's pretty awful when people take something that belongs to us. It's not right. We get angry, don't we? I do.

Jesus flipped tables that day to say, "This isn't right. Flip your focus back to God." Jesus got angry, and it showed us how much He cared.

Do you know that anger is always a second emotion? Anger is like an iceberg. You only see the top part, but underneath, there are many more emotions: fear, abandonment, loneliness, betrayal, resentment, concern, and so on.

Some people like to point to this passage and focus on Jesus's actions and anger as permission to do the same. But this was much more a heart check than an anger-permission moment. Jesus did not just flip out. **He flipped tables to flip their focus.**

That temple was destroyed. Today, the temple is you and me. It is our hearts. It is our lives.

Is there anything in your heart that Jesus needs to flip to get your focus back on God Almighty?

Where has your heart been robbed of the joy of the Lord?

Where has your faith been hijacked by distraction?

Where has sin crept in and taken up residence?

Do you need Jesus to flip a table in your heart **to make room for something else**? Something new? Something that God desires?

A heart of forgiveness?

Joy amid struggle?

Patience with your people?

Self-control in an area of temptation?

Jesus can flip these tables in our hearts. It is a treasure trove when He does. Sometimes, we might ask Him to do it; sometimes, He does it when we least expect it. Because He cares so much.

He is a Good Teacher. He is a Good Shepherd. And He's a good Table Flipper.

Where do you need Jesus to flip a table in your heart? Write out a prayer and invite Him to do so.

Let's end with a time of worship singing "I Believe" with Phil Wickham.

WEEK 3 FOCUS VERSE: LEARN IT AND LIVE IT.

Try filling in the blanks to help you learn the verse.

Praise be to the _____ and _____ of our Lord _____

_____! In his great _____ he has given us new _____

into a living _____ through the _____ of

_____ _____ from the dead.

(1 Peter 1:3)

DAY 5: FISHERMAN'S HARVEST

I love to garden. If I could rip out everything in my yard to make it grow food, I would. But my husband doesn't agree, so I take what space I can get to plant fruit trees, fruit vines, and vegetables. Since I live in Southern California, I'm blessed to have some fun produce I never had when I lived in the Midwest. Pomegranates. Avocados. Oranges. But I have a special arrangement with God. I prep the soil, lay out the water lines, put the plants in the ground, put some insect repellent around, and then hand the reigns over to God—*Your turn. Make 'em grow, God.*

The growing is always a fight that makes Genesis 2 come alive to me. Weeds. Rabbits. Possums. Aphids. Weird white powder on the leaves. Goodness. Everything seems to be against my plants. Growing things takes a lot of work and intentionality—just like our spiritual life. Left unattended, the world comes in and wreaks havoc. It takes constant vigilance, care, and intentional focus to grow spiritually.

Peter wrote:

> **Be alert** and of sober mind. Your enemy the devil prowls around like a roaring lion looking for someone to devour. Resist him, **standing firm in the faith**.

> *(1 Peter 5:8-9, emphasis added)*

Yikes. That is a good warning for us, isn't it? Pay attention and know that we have a very real enemy that wants to destroy our spiritual lives. There are so many distractions around us that Satan can use to get us focused on anything and everything but God.

It takes constant vigilance, care, and intentional focus to grow spiritually.

What are some of the distractions you are facing right now?

Today, we will look at one of the plants that Jesus focused on. We already spent some time in Mark 11 yesterday being introduced to that fig tree, but today we will return to it and focus on what happened with the tree. Jesus spoke to the fig tree before he headed to the temple in Jerusalem, where He flipped the tables. But then He returned to the tree later.

Fig tree growing
among ruins

Read Mark 11:12-14. How was Jesus feeling?

What did Jesus see in the distance? What did He do?

What did Jesus find? What season was it for the tree?

What did Jesus say to the tree?

Sometimes, this is considered a passage highlighting Jesus's anger and wrath, but Mark did not write that Jesus was angry, only that he spoke to the tree.[1] The words seem harsh and out of character for the kind, compassionate Jesus whom we know and love, but perhaps they were not.

Who heard Jesus talk to the tree?

Have you ever enjoyed:

____ Fresh figs ____ Fig bars ____ Fig glaze

____ Dried figs ____ Fig jam ____ Figs are not for me

Fig trees are native to the region, and they like dry and sunny locations. They are glorious because they produce both food and shade for this hot Mediterranean region.

These large trees grow to be twenty to twenty-three feet in height and have large leaves. Figs are teardrop-shaped fruits that start green, ripen to purplish brown, and become sweet inside.[2]

There are typically two crops of figs each year. The first crop develops in the spring on the previous year's shoot growth and is often enjoyed fresh off the tree. The second crop develops on the current year's shoot growth and ripens in late summer or fall. In the first century, that crop was dried to be enjoyed during the winter. When the Israelites were given this land by God as the Promised Land, the spies brought back figs to display some of the splendor of the land to the people.[3]

> When they reached the Valley of Eshkol, they cut off a branch bearing a single cluster of grapes. Two of them carried it on a pole between them, along with some pomegranates and **figs.**
>
> (Numbers 13:23, emphasis added)

What does Genesis 3:7 say Adam and Eve used to cover themselves in the garden of Eden when they realized they were naked after they had sinned?

The tree we read about in Mark 11 was likely found in the wild along the path to Jerusalem. Fig trees were literally and symbolically used through Scripture to talk about prosperity and judgment. Figs were vital to the people for food and the economy. When things were going well for Israel, the fig tree described this prosperity.

Read 1 Kings 4:25. What did each man have?

Read Jeremiah 5:17. What did this prophet of the Old Testament use as a symbol to describe the behavior of the people who were not honoring God?

After Jesus walked toward this fig tree and talked to it, He continued His journey to Jerusalem, where He upended the tables in the temple courts. Then, He and the disciples headed back out of the city and returned to Bethany. That was their second trip into the city. Remember the first trip was when Jesus rode in on the back of the donkey, and the people waved palm fronds shouting, "Hosanna!"

Let's pick up the story in Mark on the third day.

Read Mark 11:20-21. What did Peter, the other disciples, and Jesus see as they walked along the path and headed back into Jerusalem?

What did Peter say after he saw that the tree had withered?

Read Matthew 15:13. What did Jesus say would happen?

Read Hebrews 12:13. How did the author warn his readers?

Contrast the unhealthy roots with places in Scripture that talk about healthy roots. Which of these texts below speaks to your heart the most today? What impacts you about it?

- Ephesians 3:16-18
- Romans 11:6
- Romans 15:12
- Colossians 2:6-7
- Romans 11:18
- Revelation 22:16

Roots reach below the surface. We don't often look at them, so we don't think about them much. Instead, we tend to focus on the parts we see: the beautiful leaves, the delicious fruit, the nutritious vegetables, or the splendor of colorful flowers on display for all the world to see. But underneath the beauty is the system God created, doing much of the work. Roots absorb water and minerals to send to the rest of the plant. The roots anchor a plant in the ground to give it the support it needs to grow vertically into the air. Root systems also store food for the plants to be continuously fed. If a root system gets damaged, the plant likely will not survive.

Our support system for life is to be anchored in Jesus. We must be firmly attached to Jesus to provide all the nutrients we need to produce a fruitful life pleasing to God. Instead of fruit to eat, God wants us to grow fruit that benefits our spiritual and relational lives.

List the fruit of the Spirit found in Galatians 5:22-23. Put a star next to the one that you need Jesus to cultivate more in your life.

_____   _____

_____   _____

_____   _____

_____

The fig tree withered from the root system. Jesus spoke to the leaves because they had no fruit, but the tree died because of the root system. Jesus offered a warning and an opportunity for people to focus on fruit that was pleasing to God.

Let's contrast the fruit of the Spirit with perhaps what Jesus saw in the temple and the religious leaders:

Love > Hate   Goodness > Evil
Joy > Depression   Gentleness > Roughness
Peace > Anxiety   Faithfulness > Betrayal
Patience > Restlessness Self-Control > Indulgence
Kindness > Meanness

What stands out to you about the fruit that is evidence of the Holy Spirit and the shadow behaviors of sin that run rampant in our world?

Let's end today in worship with Tasha Layton by singing "Look What You've Done."

Write out a prayer about what is on your heart. What kind of roots and harvest do you want? Are you on course to live that out?

WEEK 3 FOCUS VERSE: LEARN IT AND LIVE IT.

Try filling in the blanks to see if you have learned this verse this week.

Praise be to the _____ and _____ of our Lord _____

_____! In his great _____ he has given us new _____

into a living _____ through the _____ of

_____ _____ from the dead.

(1 Peter 1:3)

Video Viewer Guide: *Week 3*

_____ is the view that God is everything and everyone and that everyone and everything is God.

Jesus usually referred to Himself as the Son of _____.

The title that Peter gives Jesus is *Son of* _____.

Jesus had become their _____ _____.

The word *Messiah* comes from a Hebrew word that means

_____ _____.

The word *Christ* is the Greek word that means _____ _____.

Jesus promises us that His church will _____ to the end of the age.

> You must make your choice. Either this man was, and is, the Son of God, or else a madman or something worse. You can shut him up for a fool, you can spit at him and kill him as a demon or you can fall at his feet and call him Lord and God.
> C. S. Lewis, *Mere Christianity*

Jesus is _____.

LEARN with LISA

Discussion Questions: *Week 3*

Think about these questions as you prepare to meet with your small group.

- What is your faith background?

- When did you first come to know Jesus?

- What stands out to you about the account of Peter proclaiming Jesus to be the Messiah in Caesarea Philippi?

- Who in your life needs to know the truth of who Jesus is?

- What is one thing that you would like your group to pray for you this week?

lead with compassion

Write down how you can encourage someone in your small group this week. When will you pray for them? When will you text them?

Hey Friend!

I am remembering who is dear to your heart from our discussion.

Lord, I lift up this person to you and pray you would reveal yourself in a powerful way to them today.

Perfectly
FLAWED
and
HUMBLE

(Peter Denied Jesus)

FOCUS *Verse*

Humble yourselves, therefore, under God's mighty hand, that he may lift you up in due time. Cast all your anxiety on him because he cares for you.

(1 Peter 5:6-7)

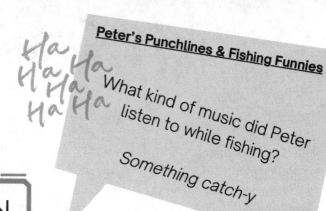

TAKE ACTION

Who is someone you think is humble? Can you model their behavior as an example? Listen more than you talk. Pick one person to express gratitude to every day.

Serve
At a school.

HUMBLE

Creation Corner

Find some flowers to enjoy. Do you have some in your garden? Visit a botanical garden or pick up a bouquet to enjoy from a grocery store. Each flower is rich in color, fragrance, and form. If God cares enough to make each of these delicate beauties, how much more does He care about you?
Read Luke 12:22-31.

C R E A T E

Create a vision board. Cut out words and images from magazines that inspire you. Decoupage them onto a papier-mache box or poster board to motivate you.

A Word from Peter

I spent a lot of time mending fishing nets. Next to my boat, my nets were the most essential tools for my work. The nets were made of linen, which is our most common fabric. After every evening of fishing, we would clean and dry the nets in the morning sun. If we didn't care for our nets, they would quickly get slimy, rot, and become useless. Andrew and I spent time during the day putting net weights on the bottom of our nets. These small pieces of stone had holes that we drilled in them and then tied them to the bottom of our nets to help them sink beneath the fish.

We used lots of different kinds of nets—including the seine, cast, and trammel—but the seine net was our go-to. It was several hundred feet long and could be twenty feet tall. We would drop this net from our boat hundreds of feet out from shore. The wood floats on one end would keep the edge on the surface and the stone weights would sink the other edge to the bottom. When we dragged our nets toward shore, that is where we would scoop up all the fish in our path. We threw out anything that didn't follow our Jewish food laws (anything without fins and scales).

I had my circular cast net when I met Jesus. This net was about twenty feet wide. And sometimes, I worked with my trammel nets. The trammels had three layers or walls of nets. Each one reinforced the other with a smaller weave. Fish passed through each layer until they found themselves caught against the inner wall, trapped. Then the fun began as we hauled that net in and found all the fish.

We used the trammels mostly at night with multiple boats. We'd throw a cast net into the center, then I often jumped out into the water to get the cast net and catch the fish trapped in the center of the larger trammels.

Holes in our nets were obviously necessary for the water to pass through, but if they were too large, then fish would escape. Sometimes, my nets would get caught on rocks, boats, or other things and tear. Sometimes, a large fish could even tear them. Hauling them in and out of the water was heavy work. I never imagined that I would lay down my hole-filled nets one day to follow a holy man. Jesus took a man who used to repair nets and showed us how He could repair hearts. He wove together broken lives to make them new. Surprisingly, I went from a life of holes to wholeness in Jesus.

Shalom,

Simon Peter

DAY 1: NAVIGATING NEW HORIZONS

At the end of the day when my kids were little, I was just so thankful that I had somehow managed to keep them alive. Little people are delightful, joy-giving, vibrant miracles…and they are exhausting. They need help in everything they do. Truly, it is a time in life when we moms must lean into God's strength when we feel weak. I have four kids, and each is completely different. Just when you think you have the hang of something, they change. Every age and stage is quite an adventure.

What words would you use to describe children? (If you don't have children, think of nieces and nephews or other important little ones in your life.) In general, how do you think they are viewed in our culture and society today?

They are little humans who are trying to figure out life. They are full of questions, energy, and emotional immaturity. (Don't you wish you could bottle that energy?)

Adults often get impatient and expect more from children than they can give. The very nature of a child is that they are immature. They are growing. They are learning. They need our help.

In the time of Jesus, children were valued and seen as a blessing from the Lord for the Hebrew community. However, they did have an insignificant social standing.[1] Let's read about how Jesus interacted with children.

Read Matthew 19:13-15. Who brought the children to Jesus?

What did the disciples do? Why do you think the disciples reacted this way?

What three things did Jesus say about children?

1.

2.

3.

How did Jesus interact with the children?

Right after this moment with the children, Jesus had a conversation with a man, one who seemed completely unrelated to His encounter with the children. Jesus is the master teacher though. He connected this man and the encounter with the children to teach Peter and the other disciples something profound. Let's see how He did it.

Read Matthew 19:16-22. What did the man ask Jesus?

> **Don't good people go to heaven and bad people go to hell? The challenge with this line of thinking is that all people do some good things and some bad things.**

Notice the man focused on what he could do to live forever. He was focused on a question that is still around today: don't good people get to have a good afterlife? Don't good people go to heaven and bad people go to hell? The challenge with this line of thinking is that all people do some good things and some bad things.[2]

Jesus focused on the word *good* that the man used. When Jesus responded to the man, He separated the man's question into two different topics. Can you identify them?

1.

2.

The first is this idea of goodness.

Let's read some places in Scripture that identify God as good. What stands out to you in these verses?

- Psalm 100:5
- Psalm 118:1, 29
- Psalm 119:68

Most of us, at some point in our lives, have questioned the goodness of God. Can you think of a time that you have done that? Why do you think that God's goodness comes into question when we are in a difficult place?

Enjoy some worship with Crowder and sing "Good God Almighty."

Jesus focused on a good God as the one who has a good plan for us to follow.

But the man also had questions about how to obtain eternal life: *How can I live forever? Is there a fountain of youth? What is the secret?*

Just as today, many views about life after death existed in Jesus's day. As religious leaders, the Pharisees taught that bodies would be resurrected. They believed and taught a literal resurrection of the physical body, which would be reunited with one's spirit. The Pharisees held firmly to oral tradition and the Torah (the first five books of the Old Testament). This allowed them to have wider interpretations of Scripture and Jewish practice than some of the other leadership sects.[3]

The Essenes and Sadducees were religious leaders who taught that there would be no resurrection of our bodies. These two sects of Judaism held to a literal view of the Torah. Since it did not mention the afterlife, they believed there was no resurrection. They believed that souls lived on but without a body.[4]

What do you believe will happen to your body and soul when you die?

Let's see what Jesus had to say about this.

Read Matthew 19:17.

Jesus talked about the reality of entering into a new life, a different life from the present one here on earth.

Read Matthew 25:46. What were the two options Jesus presented for this next life?

1.

2.

What did Jesus tell the man that he needed to do if he wanted to enter eternal life?

The Greek word used for *life* in Matthew 25:46 is ζωή, pronounced "zōē." It can mean either physical life or spiritual life.[5] Which do you think that Jesus was referring to?

The man asked which commandments he should keep. Jesus started to list the Ten Commandments, which God gave to Moses (Exodus 20), and the man said he had kept them. What else must he do?

What three things did Jesus tell this man that he must do in Matthew 19:21?

1.

2.

3.

If the man did the first two, what would he have?

Write out Matthew 6:2 in the margin.

How does our heart follow where we spend our money?

What core issue in this man's life (Matthew 19:21) was Jesus trying to help him focus on that would help him make the change he needed to become more God-focused rather than self-focused?

How do you think your relationship with material possessions impacts your relationship with God?

Read Mark 8:36-37. What does it mean to gain the world and lose your soul?

Read Matthew 19:23-26. What did Jesus say to his disciples about the rich?

Do you think this Jesus's comment is more about money or the heart?

To some, wealthier people seem to have the resources to make life more comfortable. The wealthy do not have to stress over unpaid bills, repairs, or broken appliances. They can use money to fill in all the gaps. From the outside looking in, it sure seems to make life easier.

So here was Jesus, taking something of this world that seemed to make life easier and saying that it actually made representing the kingdom of God harder. He used a shocking, silly visual illustration of the largest animal in the region, a camel, going through the most miniature everyday household item, the eye of a needle. Maybe Jesus was lightening the mood with this absurd image, or maybe Jesus was just trying to shock them.[6]

The disciples responded to the conversation with confusion. They realized most people's hearts valued their possessions and would be hesitant to give up their stuff. It felt impossible for anyone to do that. In the ancient world, and even today, wealth was seen as a blessing from God.

What did Peter and the disciples ask in Matthew 19:25?

In the margin, write out what Jesus said in Matthew 19:26.

Jesus had just created a scenario that seemed impossible. A camel through the eye of a needle. That cannot happen. No one can do that. Yet what did Jesus say that God can do?

What feels impossible to you right now?

Write in big letters over what you just wrote: POSSIBLE.

How many things is God able to make possible?

_____ A few things   _____ Most things   _____ A lot of things

_____ Some things   _____ Many things   _____ All things

Peter seemed to be tracking here. He was taking in all that Jesus had said about leaving all material things behind for the sake of the kingdom of God. After all, he gave up not only his profession and left his possessions, but he also traveled without his wife. Peter had left all things for Jesus. So Peter had a question for Jesus.

Read Matthew 19:27. What did Peter want to know?

Peter was looking for a reward.

Read Matthew 19:28-30.

A few verses before (Matthew 19:13-15), Jesus had just talked about the kingdom of heaven belonging to children. There is a contrast between those who trust in the things of this world and children who don't get to own anything. Children are entirely dependent upon those who take care of them. A rich person is self-sufficient and does not have so many needs. But those who give up things to follow Jesus will be honored by God and receive eternal life in heaven. This is the upside-down kingdom where the first will be last, and the last will be first, if they serve God with their whole hearts.

In the margin, write out Luke 9:23.

What words did you think of at the beginning of our study today that described children? Can you use those same words in a prayer to God, inviting Him to be at work to help you reflect those qualities in your walk with God?

WEEK 4 FOCUS VERSE: LEARN IT AND LIVE IT.

Try filling in the blanks to help you learn the verse. You can look back if you need some help. Practice each day, and pretty soon you will have it. The Holy Spirit will activate it in your head and heart right when you need to hear from God most.

Humble _____, therefore, under God's _____

_____, that he may _____ you up in due _____. Cast all

your _____ on him because he _____ for you.

(1 Peter 5:6-7)

DAY 2: ANCHORED IN LOVE

One of my favorite things to do at a garden store is to find the clearance area where plants that are not doing so well have been put aside. They get marked down, and I love a good deal. But there is also something rewarding in seeing a plant come back to life after it's endured some trauma.

I transplanted a little guava tree in my yard about a year ago. It looked dead for almost a year. I was just getting ready to pull it out and was completely surprised when I walked by it a few days ago. There is new life. Green leaves have sprouted out of that dead-looking wood. Amazing!

That is what Jesus can do in our lives too. He can enliven a new creation in us by His love when we least expect it. Paul wrote a verse that reflects this, one I love so much that I think about it all the time—it is a powerful affirmation of our identity in Christ. "Therefore, if anyone is in Christ, the new creation has come: The old has gone, the new is here!" (2 Corinthians 5:17). You are not who the world says you are; you are who Christ says you are.

Peter and the disciples had given up so much to follow Jesus. They were learning, they were growing, they were changing. Their old lives were distant memories as they each were becoming a new creation in Christ.

You are not who the world says you are; you are who Christ says you are.

Read John 15:9-17. How did the Father feel about His Son, Jesus?

How did Jesus feel about Peter and the disciples?

What did Jesus want them to keep just as He has kept them? If they did this, what would happen? Why is this important?

What commandment and example did Jesus give them?

What was Jesus preparing to do as He began His journey to the cross?

Whom did Jesus say are His friends?

What are some of your favorite attributes of your friends?

Do you feel the same way about your relationship with Jesus?
Why or why not?

What did Jesus call Peter and the other disciples instead of
servants?

What a powerful word. Not students. Not servants. Not followers. Friends.

What had Jesus shared with Peter and the other disciples?

What did Jesus want Peter and the other disciples to do?

As Jesus began His journey to the cross, He had a special meal with his
dearest friends, the disciples. It was the last that they shared together.

Read John 13:1. What celebration was happening in Jerusalem?

The Passover was the time of year when God had commanded the Hebrew
nation to gather and remember the account of God rescuing them out of

slavery in Egypt. It was during the first Passover that the blood of lambs was the marker that saved households from death that passed over Egypt.

What did Jesus know as He sat with Peter and the other disciples at this Passover meal?

How did Jesus feel about Peter and the other disciples?

Read John 13:2-3. What happened to the disciple Judas? What had God given to Jesus?

If all power was given to Jesus, what could Jesus have done when people came to kill Him?

Instead, Jesus remained obedient to the mission that God had for Him. Do you remember what Jesus said was true love, true friendship? Jesus honored His Father and showed love by laying down His life for His friends.

Where had Jesus come from? Where was Jesus heading?

Read John 13:4-17. Why did Jesus get up from the Passover meal that He was having with Peter and the other disciples?

Washing someone's feet would happen as soon as one entered a room. This was a common practice in first-century Greco-Roman and Jewish culture. Foot washing was a part of daily cleansing, religious purification (washing before the Sabbath), or as a sign of hospitality. In a time and place where walking dusty roads was commonplace, this was a much-needed practice.

Interestingly, John tells us that Jesus did this *during* the meal. It was meant to display His love and service to His friends, the disciples.[1] Jesus's selfless action of foot-washing also served as a strong contrast to the selfish heart the devil stirred in Judas to betray Jesus for money.

What did Peter ask Jesus in John 13:6? What tone do you envision Peter using?

What did Jesus say would happen later for Peter after Jesus washed Peter's feet?

How did Peter respond to what Jesus said to him?

Many ancient sources indicate that foot washing was reserved for those beneath your social class. When a wife washed her husband's feet, children their parents' feet, or pupils' their teachers' feet, it showed extreme devotion and honor. Since this activity had social implications, those with a higher social class did not wash the feet of those in a lower class. When Jesus took off his outer clothing and wrapped a towel around Himself to wash the feet of Peter and the other disciples, He adopted the posture of a servant or slave.[2]

This is one place in Scripture where we see Jesus clearly modeling the idea of servant-leadership. Almost all leaders in the time of Jesus adopted a "you should serve me" mentality. This idea of the leader humbling himself to a task far beneath him was revolutionary. Peter and the other disciples were likely indignant on behalf of Jesus. He was the Son of God, the promised Messiah, the King of kings, the Lord of lords—one they wanted to serve.

How do you think Jesus's example of servant-leadership shaped Peter and the other disciples as early church leaders?

Jesus was "cleaning" their outward bodies, but He wanted to communicate something deeper: He was able to clean their hearts, souls, and minds. Deep healing and cleansing were part of the work of Jesus.

Peter likely thought back to this moment many times. After the resurrection of Jesus and the launch of the disciples to share the Gospel, Peter was given a vision from God that talked about food being clean that had previously been unclean.

Read Acts 10:9-16.

Peter was given a powerful vision of food with a deeper meaning about extending the gospel to the Gentiles beyond the Jewish nation. Food that had previously been unclean (meaning they could not eat it according to Torah), God now called clean (they could now eat it). I can only wonder if these words of Jesus from this particular moment came back to Peter as he pondered the meaning of what God now called clean.

You do not realize now what I am doing, but later you will understand.

(John 13:7)

Jesus was on His way to the cross to clean up our sin mess. He would also resurrect to invite us to follow a *living* God who would extend resurrection power to us. With the power of the Spirit of God, Jesus invited the unclean to become clean. He did it for the lepers, the woman with the blood issue, and the Samaritans. The invitation grew wider every day. Jesus offers the same for us today.

How do you feel about your soul being cleaned by the work of Jesus on the cross?

Jesus created a learning environment for the disciples to experience a leadership lesson in self-sacrifice, self-giving love, and servanthood. These were to become defining attributes of the community He called them to develop.

Now that I, your Lord and Teacher, have washed your feet, you also should wash one another's feet. I have set you an example that you should do as I have done for you.

(John 13:14-15)

Jesus's actions of love, loyalty, and sacrifice were contrasted with those of Judas, who chose to betray, reject, and sin.

Read John 13:17-30. In John 13:27-29, what were some things the disciples thought Judas might have been doing when Jesus said, "What you are about to do, do quickly"?

Once the betrayal was set in motion, there was a transition. The time had come, and Jesus shifted into the next phase of his mission. It was time to begin the journey to the cross.

Read John 13:31-38. What word do you see the most in John 13:31-32?

The Greek word for glory that was used in these verses was δοξάζω, pronounced "doxazō."[3] It means to give praise and honor to someone or something. The journey to the cross would be filled with pain, sacrifice, and suffering—but also glory.

Write out the new command Jesus gave Peter and the other disciples.

What did Peter ask Jesus?

Jesus told Peter that he could not follow where He was going, which confused Peter. After all, he had followed Jesus in a lot of places. He had followed Jesus into boats and out of boats. He had followed Jesus into homes and onto roads. He followed Jesus into countless synagogues and the temple courts. He had followed Jesus through doubts, fears, and confusion. He was in. He would follow Jesus anywhere.

Worship and proclaim the truth that you are a child of God. Sing with Chris Tomlin "Jesus Loves Me."

Write out the commitment that Peter offered to Jesus in John 13:37.

Jesus gave Peter some disturbing news. What did Jesus say Peter was going to do?

If you have ever experienced rejection, Jesus understands. He left a message of lasting love, commitment, and sacrifice as the message for His followers and the hope for the church. He anchors you in love.

Read Matthew 26:31-35 for Matthew's account of this event. What stands out to you?

Open handedly invite Jesus in a time of prayer to reveal to you who you could serve in a sacrificial way today that would reveal the deep love of Jesus. Write down what you hear from the Lord.

WEEK 4 FOCUS VERSE: LEARN IT AND LIVE IT.

Try filling in the blanks to help you learn the verse.

Humble _____, therefore, under God's _____ _____, that he may _____ you up in due _____. Cast all your _____ on him because he _____ for you.

(1 Peter 5:6-7)

DAY 3: STORMY SEAS

Some of the most famous swords today are the ones that never existed—King Arthur's Excalibur, Aragorn's Anduril, and Luke Skywalker's lightsaber. These weapons have kept us on the edge of our seats in the fight of good against evil in novels and on the big screen. They are legendary. They are powerful. They are even inspirational.

But there is another sword that tells a significant story. This sword played a part in the events leading up to the cross. As the crucifixion of Jesus approached, moments seemed to fall in rapid succession, piling upon one another, each appalling, horrific, and heartbreaking.

> Read Matthew 26:36-46. Where did Jesus go with His disciples after the Last Supper?

Ironically, on this night of violence, Jesus was never about a political or military revolt, much to the disappointment of Jewish expectation.[1] He had not come to pierce the political regime but rather to pierce our souls with grace, truth, hope, and life.

> Read John 18:1. What was the place where Jesus was with Peter and the disciples?

| _____ Road | _____ Home | _____ River |
| _____ Inn | _____ Garden | _____ Mountain |

Gethsemane is from the Hebrew/Aramaic word _gat šemanim_, which means "oil press." Gethsemane was likely a grove of olive trees on the Mount of Olives. Olives were either eaten or crushed to prepare olive oil for cooking and anointing. Large stone olive presses would be nearby to crush the harvested olives.[2]

Today, if you visit Israel, there is a garden with a grove of very old olive trees where you can go and remember this moment in Scripture.

You can stand among the olive trees that are hundreds of years old and remember how Jesus was pressed to the near breaking point with sorrow and grief yet remained faithful.

Jesus had not come to pierce the political regime but rather to pierce our souls with grace, truth, hope, and life.

Left photo: Historic olive trees in the garden of Gethsemane

Right photo: Part of an ancient oil press found in the national park in Gamla, Israel

As the kings of old were anointed with olive oil, Jesus was anointed as the King of kings by God Himself. Jesus was pressed and yet persevered.

Where do you feel called today to persevere despite being squeezed like an olive?

What did Jesus go to the garden of Gethsemane to do? How did He feel? Whom did He take with Him?

What did Jesus ask Peter, James, and John to do?

What did Jesus ask of God, His Father, in Matthew 26:39?

Read the prayer Jesus taught Peter and the disciples to pray in Matthew 6:9-13. What words are repeated in this prayer from the one that Jesus just prayed?

What were Peter, James, and John doing when Jesus returned to them?

_____ Eating   _____ Gambling   _____ Praying

_____ Arguing   _____ Preaching   _____ Sleeping

In Matthew 26:40, whom did Jesus directly speak to with frustration?

Jesus went back and prayed a second time. What did Jesus ask of God His Father in Matthew 26:42?

When Jesus returned to Peter, James, and John this time, what were they doing?

What do you notice in common about the number of times that Jesus repeated this prayer pattern, the number of times Jesus asked God if there was another way?

The number three in Scripture is like an exclamation point. It is a repetition factor meant to catch our attention and emphasize something that God wants us to pay attention to.

When my daughter was little and wanted my attention, she would pull my face away from my laptop or phone and say, "Look at me, Mommy." Even my little puppy has learned to put her paws on my computer and push it away to get me to pay attention to her. They know when I am not giving them my full attention and have learned how to ask or *demand* it.

The number three in Scripture is a wake-up call to pay attention. If you missed it the first time, pay attention the second. If you missed it the second time, you get one more chance. Pay attention.

Read John 18:1-11. How did Judas know where to find Jesus?

Whom did Judas bring with him?

1.

2.

3.

What were they carrying with them?

1.

2.

3.

How did Jesus feel about Judas's actions? (Hint: John 18:4)

What three words did Jesus use to identify Himself two times?

Read Exodus 3:14. How does God identify Himself?

Why do you think this group fell to the ground when Jesus identified Himself using these well-known sacred words as a title?

What did Jesus request of the group that had come to arrest Him?

How did Peter react to the group wanting to arrest Jesus?

It was a tense night with a crowd out for blood, carrying clubs and swords. They did not expect Jesus to go peacefully. They expected a battle. The weapons carried that night were common for short-range combat in the first century. Israel was a nation occupied by Roman rule, Roman soldiers, and Roman weapons.

We may find it strange that Peter was armed that night. He was obviously ready for a fight, but his sword was not the deadliest weapon that night. It was the kiss of betrayal, the abandonment of the disciples, the lies of the religious leaders, the brutality of the soldiers, and the manipulation of Pilate.

We all carry weapons. Weapons of betrayal, lies, anger, selfishness, blame. At least Peter's weapon was easy to see—unlike the weapons we often carry. Sometimes, we wound people even when we thought we were doing the right thing.

Peter's motive was the protection of his friend, of his Lord. He used his sword to defend Jesus. I don't blame him. I admire his passion. His zeal. His righteous anger. He disregards his own life so that he could try to save another. Peter tried to save Jesus even as Jesus was about to save him. Peter was brought to the edge of devotion for his Lord.

The actual blade Peter used, wherever it ended up, found its mark that night. In the crowd that pushed in around the disciples was Malchus, a servant of the high priest, Caiaphas, who had organized the plot to kill Jesus. Joseph Caiaphas was the Roman-appointed Jewish high priest, and he sent Malchus to watch and listen. Malchus was to report back to Caiaphas what happened with Jesus.[3] He was the ear of Caiaphas on that eventful evening. He sought to establish a charge of blasphemy and, eventually, treason against Jesus.

As high priest, Caiaphas was the most powerful Jew in the land.[4] He did not like Jesus or His message. As a servant, Malchus's life was not his own. His master was corrupt and crafty. He threw Malchus into the fray to spy for him, and Malchus was the one who caught Peter's wrath.

Peter likely swung at whoever was closest to him in the armed mob around them. Peter probably thrust his sword with a mortal wound in mind. But he wasn't a soldier. He was a fisherman, and he missed. But not completely. He cut off Malchus's ear. It must have happened so quickly that there was little time to think. Peter and Malchus were both likely in shock as they stared at the ear lying on the ground, blood flowing.

Read Luke 22:49-51. What did Jesus say to Peter after he cut off Malchus's ear?

What did Jesus do for Malchus?

Jesus had healed so many. He had healed lepers and restored skin to health. He had healed the blind and given back their sight. He had healed the mute and given back their voice. He had healed the lame and given back their mobility. The last miracle of Jesus's ministry before going to the cross was to heal Malchus. He reached out and touched his ear. In moments, Malchus had gone from hunting Jesus to being healed by Jesus.

With his adrenaline flowing from the attack, Peter must have stood amazed at the actions of Jesus. Maybe, he was even annoyed. Why did Jesus always do that? Jesus loved everyone—even his enemies—demonstrating that there is no healing without compassion, no restoration without love.

As Malchus touched his restored ear that had lain on the ground only seconds earlier, he was faced with deciding who he would now turn his ears toward. The man they called "the ear of Caiaphas" had encountered the Son of God. He had been healed by Jesus of Nazareth. The very one Malchus had been sent to arrest *had cured him*.[5]

Jesus may not have held the sword, but He had a powerful way of cutting out the hate in Peter and cutting out the pain of Malchus. Jesus replaced them with love. Jesus called Peter to lay down his sword.

"You have heard that it was said, 'Love your neighbor and hate your enemy.' But I tell you, love your enemies and pray for those who persecute you, that you may be children of your Father in heaven." (Matthew 5:43-45)

Do you have a sword that you need to lay down today? Where do you need the compassion of Jesus to fill you?

Make a list telling God which places in your life are in stormy seas, times when you feel betrayed, angry, and defensive. Why do you think these people and events have impacted you so deeply? Have you cut off any of these relationships? Invite Jesus to begin the work of emotional healing.

When I have felt betrayed:	When I have become angry:	When I have become defensive:

Why was this painful?	What was the emotion I felt before anger?	What do I need to defend?

WEEK 4 FOCUS VERSE: LEARN IT AND LIVE IT.

Try filling in the blanks to help you learn the verse.

Humble _____, therefore, under God's _____

_____, that he may _____ you up in due _____. Cast all

your _____ on him because he _____ for you.

(1 Peter 5:6-7)

Let's end our time today in worship with Casting Crowns and sing "Healer."

DAY 4: TIDES OF TREACHERY

CODE NAME: GREYSUIT

Photo courtesy of Wikimedia Commons

On February 18, 2001, Robert Hanssen headed home after dropping a friend off at the airport. As he drove home to Vienna, Virginia, he stopped at Foxstone Park. He exited the car that cold evening and stuck a piece of white medical tape on the sign outside the park entrance. Then, he walked through the park on that winter day to the wooden footbridge and placed a sealed black garbage bag in a secret spot near the base of the bridge. Looking around to make sure he was unseen, he quickly but inconspicuously darted back to the safety of his car. But that night was different; someone had been watching and waiting. After twenty years of Hanssen selling American secrets to Russia, the FBI had finally caught up with him.[1]

He was swarmed by a team of FBI agents, all armed and ready to take action against this American spy. As they placed handcuffs on Hanssen, he had only one question: "What took you so long?"[2]

It was a question filled with the arrogance of a traitor who had profited from lies and deception for years. Hanssen collected an estimated $1.4 million for giving lists of American undercover agents abroad, revealing the identities of Russian double agents, providing documents showing the US intercepting Soviet transmissions, and giving Russia the methods by which the US would retaliate in the event of a nuclear attack.

The Department of Justice called the work of Robert Hanssen "possibly the worst intelligence disaster in US history." Sentenced to fifteen consecutive life sentences without parole, Hanssen died in a Colorado supermax prison in 2023.[3] How does someone born in Chicago, Illinois, with an MBA and working as an accountant become this treacherous? How does one person do so much damage?

After working as an accountant, Hanssen joined the Chicago Police Department as an internal affairs investigator specializing in forensic accounting. In January 1976, he left the police department to join the FBI. Only three years after joining the FBI, he was caught spying for the Soviet Union, not by the FBI but by his wife. She found him secretly copying documents in the basement of their home. When she asked him about it, he lied and said he was tricking the Russians and giving them false information. But he was not tricking the Russians; he was tricking the Americans.[4]

It reads like a good spy movie, doesn't it? The stuff of novels and TV. In fact, they made his story into a movie in 2007 called *Breach*. But this story wasn't made up; it was real. Lives were ruined because of one man's betrayal. It's a heartbreaking story because he was also a family man, married with six kids. He was a devout Catholic and went on vacations to Florida to visit their grandmother.[5] No one knew the darkness lurking in his heart. Tragically, he made a series of bad decisions that led to the deep betrayal of his country.

When we think of betrayal in the Bible, we often focus on Judas. He betrayed Jesus by accepting a bribe and bringing the soldiers to where Jesus was located on that fateful night, identifying Jesus with a kiss.

Read Luke 22:52-54. What happened to Jesus? Where did they take Him? Who followed them from a distance?

Read Luke 22:55-62. What did Peter do when people built a fire?

Who recognized Peter? What did Peter say when that person said that Peter had been with Jesus?

Read Matthew 26:71-72. Who was the next person to recognize Peter? How did Peter respond to this accusation?

Read John 18:26-27. Who accused Peter a third time?

Read Matthew 26:73-75. How did Peter respond to this third round of accusations?

What happened immediately after Peter denied Jesus three times?

Read Luke 22:61. What happened after that piercing sound rang through the morning air? How did Peter respond to this moment?

How do you think Peter felt?

How is denying you know someone an act of betrayal?

Betrayal is one of the most painful actions people experience because it is usually done by someone known and trusted. Betrayal is relational. The closer you are to someone, the more devastating it feels when they betray you.

Have you ever pretended that you didn't know someone? Or has someone pretended not to know you?

Betrayal is so difficult because it is the act of breaking trust. Betrayal says or does something that breaks a promise. Betrayal chooses selfish desires over and above the relationship.

Betrayal is one of the most painful actions people experience because it is usually done by someone known and trusted. Betrayal is relational. The closer you are to someone, the more devastating it feels when they betray you. You don't feel the same if an acquaintance lies to you versus someone you have shared your life with.

When we are betrayed, it wounds us deeply because we didn't expect it. When we trust someone, we give them a piece of our heart. We are hard-wired as relational beings. We want connection, we want relationships, we want belonging. We want to trust others.

Betrayal is traumatizing because it calls into question our decision-making. We did not see the betrayal coming, so our judgment and intuition feel messed up. How can we make another decision?

When trust is shattered, you question yourself, your views, and your world. Perhaps you remember when you were betrayed by a friend, a business partner, or a spouse.

So. Hard. These betrayals can eat us up, can't they?

Are there any betrayals that still harbor pain in your heart?

The wounds of betrayal make it all the more profound and precious when we are met with someone truly loyal, trustworthy, and faithful. Someone who acts and speaks with care and protection. Someone who is trustworthy.

The crucifixion of Jesus was punctuated by so much pain and betrayal. Perhaps that allows us to appreciate more deeply what came on the other side of the cross. I cannot imagine the agonizing grief of all those who loved and trusted Jesus as they watched Him die. Peter was wracked not only with the extreme agony of the loss of a friend but also of his own behavior toward Jesus before He died.

Read Luke 23.

The darkness of betrayal was nailed to the cross that day. Jesus died so that the weapons of Satan (hate, greed, lust, pride, jealousy, deception, betrayal, etc.) would be crushed and shown less powerful than the ways of Jesus. Love won out that day. Jesus remained loyal to God.[6] Jesus invites us to remain loyal to Him because Jesus remains loyal to us.

But the Lord is faithful, and he will strengthen you and protect you from the evil one.

(2 Thessalonians 3:3)

Look up these verses that describe how God feels about loyalty and faithfulness. Write out the verse that impacts you the most today. How is the Spirit speaking to you through these words?

- Deuteronomy 31:6
- Deuteronomy 31:8
- Joshua 1:5
- 1 Kings 8:57
- Psalm 25:10
- Psalm 33:4
- Psalm 57:10
- Isaiah 25:1

Jesus can help us be loyal. Loyal to Him and loyal to people. Temptations are all around us. But for every temptation, Jesus always provides a way out.

The cross provided a way out of this evil plot filled with hate, deception, and betrayal. The cross stands firmly planted in the pages of Scripture and our lives as a symbol; a permanent, precious reminder that Jesus is loyal.

He is loyal to the mission of love. He is loyal to the reality of redeeming brokenness. He is loyal to His promise of a thousand better tomorrows. He is loyal and will lead you in this life with purpose. He is faithful. He is trustworthy. The tides of treachery with traitors, liars, deceivers, and betrayers will always be with us on this side of heaven. They will wound us, but by the power of His loyal love, they don't have to win. Love wins. Jesus wins.

Let's get our worship on with Phil Wickham singing "How Great Is Your Love."

End today in a prayer expressing to Jesus how grateful you are that He remained loyal to God's call on His life out of great love for you. Will you remain loyal to Him?

WEEK 4 FOCUS VERSE: LEARN IT AND LIVE IT.

Try filling in the blanks to help you learn the verse.

Humble _____, therefore, under God's _____ _____, that he may _____ you up in due _____. Cast all your _____ on him because he _____ for you.

(1 Peter 5:6-7)

DAY 5: WAVES OF REJUVENATION

Some people love surprises, and some people hate them. For me, it truly depends on the kind of surprise—good or bad. I love the good ones. I remember sitting in a staff meeting and almost falling off my chair when a coworker, a confirmed bachelor who had been single for more than fifty years, announced he was engaged and getting married. I had no idea he was dating someone, let alone ready to give up his single life and get married. I was shocked and happy about his joyous news.

Can you think of a time that you were truly surprised by something good?

Getting a phone call from my parents, however, that my dad had been diagnosed with untreatable stage 4 cancer was a horrible surprise I wish had never happened. It caught our whole family off guard and plunged us into a very difficult season of care and grief for him. In nine short weeks from his diagnosis, he went home to be with Jesus.

Can you think of a time that you were surprised by something bad?

The disciples of Jesus had watched in shock and deep grief as He was crucified. Even though the good surprise of the Resurrection was just around the corner, they did not know it would happen. Jesus had dropped clues during His ministry about the Resurrection, but none of them could conceive of it. After the horrific crucifixion of their beloved Lord, the community began the grief process of preparing His body for burial.

Read John 19:38-42. Who asked Pilate for the body of Jesus after He died on the cross? Who assisted this man with the preparation of Jesus's body?

These two men appear to have been secret disciples of Jesus who were ready to make a bold statement of public belief at the crucifixion.[1]

How many pounds of spices did they use to prepare the body of Jesus?

_____ 25 _____ 40 _____ 50 _____ 62 _____ 75 _____ 90

What was near the place where Jesus was crucified?

Where did these men lay the body of Jesus for burial?

I take a lot of joy in gardening. Well, not the weeds or bugs determined to eat my plants. But there is something beautiful about working with the soil, putting a seed or plant in the hidden, dark ground, and watching it slowly grow and produce fresh veggies, fruit, or a beautiful flower. It is always a spectacular surprise when the plant moves from storing all the nutrients to bursting forth with bounty.

I can't help thinking of the powerful symbolism of when they laid Jesus in a rock tomb in a garden. His body was set in a cold, dark cave, but it would soon burst forth with glorious new life that surprised the watching world.

Today, in Israel, there are a couple of locations that the church has historically preserved as possible sites of Jesus's death and resurrection. One is located at the Church of the Holy Sepulchre. This is a huge church that many saints visit to see a rock preserved as the crucifixion site. Within the church structure, there is also a rock tomb revered as Jesus's.

There is a second possible location for the crucifixion, burial, and resurrection of Jesus. It is known as the Garden Tomb, located near the Damascus Gate, and it stands in the shadow of Skull Hill. You can see photos of how the hill resembled a skull. Over the years, erosion has made it less visible. The bridge of the nose was washed out years ago, but in older photos, you can make out the outline of two eyes and a nose.

They came to a place called Golgotha (which means "the place of the skull").

(Matthew 27:33)

Today, this garden is maintained as a place that you can visit to sit, reflect, and worship. You can see an ancient empty tomb that provides a powerful experience aligned with these Scriptures.

Walking in that tomb makes me thankful for something I don't say often. "I've never been so happy to see *nothing*." It is an *empty* tomb. Hallelujah.

*Photos
(from left to right):*

Interior of the Church of the Holy Sepulchre

Skull Hill with the eyes and nose denoted for readers

The Garden Tomb

Read John 20:1-2. Who went to the tomb? What did she discover? Which disciples did she run to tell?

What day of the week was it?

Read John 20:3-10. Who reached the tomb first? Did he go into the tomb?

Who reached the tomb second? Did he go into the tomb? What did he discover?

John lists the details of the linen being left behind to indicate that there was intentionality there. The body was gone, but the grave clothes remained. If someone had come and stolen the body of Jesus, wouldn't they have also taken the grave clothes?

It was traditional in ancient Israel for the dead to be wrapped in cloth and anointed with spices for burial. Likely, Mary and the other women who went to the tomb on Sunday morning expected to prepare the body with more spices.[2] But when Mary Magdalene saw the stone rolled away, she feared someone had taken Jesus. She ran to alert Peter and John, who then responded by running to the grave.

John wrote that neither Peter, John, nor the other disciples had understood what had happened. When John said he believed, perhaps he meant that he believed Mary.[3] There is no indication of what Peter thought.

Read Matthew 28:1-15. What four things happened in Matthew 28:2?

1.

2.

3.

4.

Read Matthew 27:50-51. What also happened when Jesus died on the cross?

Read Luke 19:39-40 and then write out Luke 19:40.

When have you been silent about your faith when you wish you would have spoken up?

Jesus had told his followers that he would rise on the third day. Read these three Scriptures. What do they all have in common?

- Matthew 16:21
- Matthew 17:23
- Matthew 20:19

In Scripture, even a part of a day was counted as a whole day. Jesus was in the tomb for parts of three days. He was crucified on Friday, at approximately 3:00 p.m., just before the Sabbath began at sundown—day one. He was in the tomb during the Sabbath—day two. Then, on Sunday, He resurrected sometime in the early morning—day three. Jesus was raised on the third day, just as He had prophesied.

Jesus appeared to the women first, who then ran and told the disciples about the resurrected Jesus. The women became the first evangelists. Those whom society often hushed and ignored became the very ones whom Jesus gave the glorious news first. They didn't walk; they ran to proclaim that the tomb was empty.

John 20:10 tells us that the disciples returned to where they were staying in Jerusalem. Matthew 24:33 reports two eyewitnesses who had a conversation with Jesus and went to where the disciples were staying to tell them that what the women were saying was true.

Read Mark 16:1-7. Whom did the angel tell the women to go and tell about the risen Jesus? (Hint: Mark 16:7)

1.

2.

Read Luke 24:34. According to these men, whom did Jesus appear to?

We don't have much information other than that it was important for Jesus to identify Simon Peter as one of the first ones He wanted to know about the Resurrection. Peter was the leader of the disciples, so it was important for him to know so that he could lead this incredible transition for the team.

Yet Peter also remained in deep despair over his three denials of Jesus. He was likely overwhelmed not only by the loss of his leader, rabbi, and friend but also that his last moments with Jesus were a betrayal.

Jesus remained loyal to God, and Peter gave into fear. He chose self-protection and denial rather than alignment with Jesus to the end. Jesus, in His great mercy and compassion, cared for Peter, ready to meet him in his pain. Jesus would remain loyal to Peter and restore their relationship.

Read John 20:19-29. Whom did Jesus appear to?

What did He show them? How did the disciples feel?

Which disciple was there when Jesus first appeared to them? What did Jesus do to let him know He was alive?

What phrase did Jesus repeat when He appeared to the disciples?

Fear had likely gripped the hearts and minds of the disciples as they huddled together, waiting for the authorities to come after them and kill them just as they had Jesus. He mercifully came to them through locked doors to reveal the truth of His resurrection and to commission them for ministry.[4]

According to Mark 16:7, where would the disciples see Jesus again?

Only John reports the sweet reunion and restoration of Peter that happens in John 21. This will be the focus of our video teaching time at the end of this week. I can't wait to share Jesus's powerful restoration of Peter.

Let's look at a few more things as we finish our day together.

On what day did Jesus appear to the disciples? (Hint: John 20:19)

> **The Resurrection is what brings hope, healing, and power into our lives.**

Sunday is resurrection day. It is the first day of the week. Our weekend schedule makes it easy to think that Sunday is the last day of the week. But Sunday is the day that begins our week. It is the day that sets the tone for the rest of the week. It is resurrection day. This is why the Christian church has historically met on Sunday mornings. It is the day and time of the resurrection of Jesus. It changes everything for us. The Resurrection is what brings hope, healing, and power into our lives.

Read Ephesians 1:18-20.

What three things did Paul pray that God's people would know?

1.

2.

3.

Resurrection power is incomparable to anything else in this world, and it is extended to those who believe. Jesus gives us the same power that raised Him from the dead to be our strength when we are weak.

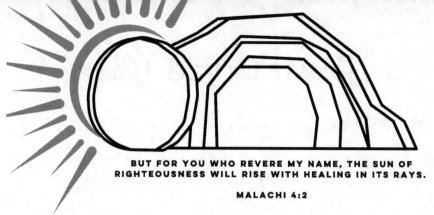

BUT FOR YOU WHO REVERE MY NAME, THE SUN OF
RIGHTEOUSNESS WILL RISE WITH HEALING IN ITS RAYS.

MALACHI 4:2

Let's get our worship on and sing "Forever" with Kari Jobe.

Highlight the part of the following verse that excites you most.

Now to him who is able to do immeasurably more than all we ask or imagine, according to his power that is at work within us, to him be glory in the church and in Christ Jesus throughout all generations, for ever and ever! Amen.

(Ephesians 3:20-21)

Draw a picture or write a prayer about how the power and joy of resurrection impact your heart, life, relationships, and future. Where does it bring waves of rejuvenation?

WEEK 4 FOCUS VERSE: LEARN IT AND LIVE IT.

Try filling in the blanks to help you learn the verse.

*Humble _____, therefore, under God's _____
_____, that he may _____ you up in due _____. Cast all
your _____ on him because he _____ for you.*

(1 Peter 5:6-7)

Video Viewer Guide: *Week 4*

Jesus served them with _____.

Peter stepped away rather than toward _____ in Christ.

This rock had _____.

Jesus had _____ from the _____.

Jesus called out their _____.

Lives with holes, or _____, could still be _____ by Jesus.

God never _____ our _____.

Peter was in the presence of the God of _____.

Discussion Questions: *Week 4*

Think about these questions as you prepare to meet with your small group.

- Who has betrayed you?

- Why do you think that betrayal is so hard to recover from?

- What stands out to you about the account of how Jesus restored Peter?

- What are some ways in which you have worked through the process of forgiveness?

- What is one thing that you would like your group to pray for you this week?

model forgiveness

Write down how you can encourage someone in your small group this week. When will you pray for them? When will you text them?

Hey Friend!

Want to meet up for lunch this week?

I'd love to hear more of your story. I am so glad you are in my group!

Perfectly FLAWED *and* EMPOWERED

(Peter Preached Jesus)

FOCUS *Verse*

His divine power has given us everything we need for a godly life through our knowledge of him who called us by his own glory and goodness.

(2 Peter 1:3)

TAKE ACTION

Write a text, email, or letter to a missionary, pastor, or person in ministry encouraging them to boldly persevere and minister in the power of the Holy Spirit.

Serve

A widow.

EMPOWERED

Creation Corner

Spend one hour (or more) outside looking for wildlife. Keep count of all you see: birds, squirrels, chipmunks, and so forth. Pay attention to your soul as you keep a vigilant lookout for wildlife. What does it want to say? Listen to what is happening deep within your soul as you watch intently for a glimpse of animals. We need soul talk more than self-talk. Read Psalm 42.

C
R
E
A
T
E

Find something for your home that has great form at a thrift store. Spray-paint it black, gold, white, or any color to empower it with a new lease on life.

A Word from Peter

Most of the time, nets were our regular work gear. But we also had spears, lines, and bronze hooks to use when needed. Just when I thought I had left those all behind, Jesus put my fishing skills back in play. I loved Jesus's sense of humor. He was the best. When we had to pay our temple taxes, He sent me back to the sea. His instructions were very specific, no nets were needed. He told me to use only one line and take the first fish I caught. Do you know what was in that little guy? A four-drachma coin! Riches from the sea! Best taxes I've ever paid. And I got a meal out of it too.

I used a simple hook that day, and I only needed one fish. Fish were hunted and trapped on those little hooks. I couldn't help thinking on the day that Jesus was crucified that those awful Roman crosses were like my fishhooks. Only they were spearing people. Jesus was pierced for all our sins. It was a sacrifice I planned to tell as many people about as possible. It broke my heart to have Jesus crucified, but it also saved my soul. I am forever grateful.

The greatest catch of all is not found in the waters of my beloved Sea of Galilee but in the boundless depths of the divine grace of my beloved Savior.

Shalom,

Simon Peter

DAY 1: A BREATH OF FRESH AIR

Peter watched Jesus as the Son of God perform many miracles that shocked, awed, healed, and delighted people. The display of power over the natural elements was a way that Jesus revealed God's authority over all things. Jesus's actions opened the door for people to pay attention to His words.

Incidentally, the Bible is full of stories about God doing miracles and people moving from wonder and belief to disbelief and disobedience. After God freed the Israelites from slavery in Egypt with ten miracles, the people shortly forgot and turned away from God. This was true for Jesus also. Even after seeing Him as a miracle worker, the people soon forgot, turned against Him, and crucified Him.

Many people want a miracle from God to prove that God exists. Would one miracle be enough? Two? Twenty? The evidence of Scripture shows us that people were only amazed for a short time and then demanded more. As soon as something scary happens and fear takes over, people's minds and spirits once again become consumed with doubt.

In this lesson, we will read about a miracle that Peter and John did while in Jerusalem. Filled with the Holy Spirit, they had been sent by Jesus to display God's power and preach the gospel.

Read Acts 3:1-5. Who was Peter with? What time was it?

Read the following two verses. What do they have in common?

- Psalm 55:17
- Daniel 6:10

The Jewish community had a regular rhythm of praying three times a day. Eventually, set times were assigned for observing these prayers: third hour—9 a.m., sixth hour—12 p.m., and nineth Hour—3 p.m.

The morning and evening prayers seemed to have coincided with the morning and evening sacrifices offered by the priests in the temple (Exodus 29:38-39; Numbers 28:2-8).[1]

> Jesus's actions opened the door for people to pay attention to His words.

Rhythms are things that you build into your routine. This is how we created healthy faith habits. One rhythm my husband and I used to teach our kids to look for God was conversation prompts around dinner. Our questions for each child were:

- What was the best part of your day?
- What was the hardest part of your day?
- Where did you see God working?

Sometimes, we'd get silly toddler answers like God is in my tummy or in my lunch box. But as the kids have gotten older, it is such a joy to hear them be able to look for God working around them in conversations, creation, and their experiences.

As Peter and John went to the temple to pray, God interrupted them. I love that they were willing to be interrupted for what God wanted to do. By paying attention to the Spirit, they could see God's power unfold before them in a pretty spectacular way. Often, my prayer is, *Lord, please let me never be too busy to be interrupted by you. Interrupt me.*

When we are aware of God's presence and promptings around us, we might just get to see His glory revealed right in front of us.

When we are aware of God's presence and promptings around us, we might just get to see His glory revealed right in front of us. Peter and John got interrupted on a routine journey to pray. They had not even started praying yet, and they got to see God's glory because they were on the lookout for God's presence to intervene. They were willing, watchful, and ready to let God work through them.

In Acts 3:2, who was carried to the temple gate? How long had he struggled with this ailment?

Why was he brought to the gate and what did he ask Peter and John for?

Have you ever been asked for this before? How do you handle the situation?

What did Peter and John do first?

They saw him. How many people do you think walked past this man on a regular basis? How do you feel when people walk past you and ignore you? Feeling invisible is a deeply demeaning experience. It causes you to wonder why you are even here on earth. Do you matter? Does anyone care?

Those who struggled with any kind of physical or mental condition were often neglected in ancient societies. Medical professionals were not highly regarded because they were poorly trained and often ineffective in treating people with diseases and ailments. Unfortunately, disabilities were often viewed as a punishment from God. When Jesus came, He completely changed this understanding.[2]

Look up these verses. Circle the one that impacted you the most today as you read it and write it below.

- Leviticus 19:14
- Deuteronomy 27:18
- Isaiah 42:16
- Proverbs 31:8-9
- Luke 14:12-14
- John 9:1-3
- Mark 7:32-35
- Mark 8:22-25

Read Acts 3:6-10. Did Peter give the man money?

_____ Yes, a lot   _____ Yes, a little   _____ No, none at all

Write out what Peter said to him:

Let's get our praise on and sing "Praise" with Elevation Worship.

What were the two things Peter did next?

1.

2.

What happened to the man?

Who did the man give credit to? How did he do this?

What was the name of the gate where all of this happened?

The temple was central in Jerusalem and was the Jewish community's main hub for religious and social life. Amazingly, King Herod built the temple in eighteen months by renovating and expanding what is called the second temple (the first was built by King Solomon and the second by Zerubbabel). The temple mount plaza was 172,222 square yards—equivalent to about twenty-nine American football fields. The walls rose ten stories high, with massive stonework underground supporting the structure.[3] Many of the gate entrances were overlaid with gold, silver, bronze, and intricate carvings. Scholars believe the name "Beautiful" was a nickname for the central Nicanor gate because of its massive size, ornate beauty, and important significance as the main entrance.[4] Rome tragically destroyed the temple in AD 70 during the first Jewish-Roman war. Today, only one retaining wall remains. This is the Western Wall, also known as the Wailing Wall. It received its nickname from the Jewish community at the time, who would weep with sorrow over the destruction.

Read Luke 21:5-6. What did Jesus predict will happen?

Write out Ecclesiastes 3:11.

What do you need for God to turn beautiful in your life?

Read Acts 3:11-16. Who did Peter say healed this man?

Read Acts 3:17-26.

With quite a confrontational accusation, Peter put substantial blame on the people for the death of Jesus.

> **You killed** the author of life, but God **raised him from the dead.** We are witnesses of this.
>
> (Acts 3:15, emphasis added)

Peter presented a powerful juxtaposition of their guilty actions and God's power as he talked to the gathered crowd. They were in awe of the miracle, but that was just the opening act. Peter pointed to the power of God that went beyond that one act on that day at the temple. He reminded them of their role in Jesus's death. Talk about an emotionally charged moment. Peter and John stood their ground with courage, determined to touch hearts and invite the crowd to respond to Jesus. It was not too late.

Write out Acts 3:16. Circle the word *faith* every time it occurs. Underline the two places that talk about Jesus's name.

Read Philippians 2:9-11 and describe how these verses speak to you about the power of the name of Jesus.

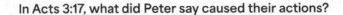

In Acts 3:17, what did Peter say caused their actions?

In Acts 3:19, Peter called them to repent and turn to God to *wipe out their sin*. Isn't that just the best description of the forgiveness of sin? Wiped out. Gone.

Look up Psalm 103:11-12. What does God do with our sins (transgressions)?

It's oooouuutttta here.

One of my sons plays baseball, and can I tell you about the excitement in that Little League field when someone hits a home run? We go bonkers, bananas. The ball goes over the fence, never to be seen again.

That is the same thrill I get when I think about how God views sin when we confess it and turn away from it (repentance).

The Greek word is ἐξαλείφω (ex-al-i'-fo), and it means "to wipe something out or obliterate it." It is to remove it as if it were never there.[5] Isn't that a life-giving breath of fresh air?

How does it make you feel to know God gives us a clean start through the power of forgiveness when we admit we are wrong?

Peter went on to talk about a time of refreshing. Where do you need God to refresh your heart for the things of the Lord? Write out a prayer asking the Holy Spirit to come upon you in a fresh way and restore, renew, and refresh you.

WEEK 5 FOCUS VERSE: LEARN IT AND LIVE IT.

It's a new week and a new verse. Start working on it and hide this treasure in your heart.

His _____ power has given us _____ we _____

for a godly _____ through our _____ of him who

_____ us by his own _____ and _____ .

(2 Peter 1:3)

DAY 2: CASTING AUTHORITY

I broke my foot the summer I was pregnant with my fourth baby. It got caught in the jaws of a wild bear while I was out camping. Just kidding. I often wish for a jaw-dropping good story about it. The truth is I was walking out of my parent's front door, and I simply made a misstep, rolled my foot, and went down. I was carrying my toddler son and performed an Oscar-worthy ninja move to protect him and my unborn child. Thankfully, they were both fine. My foot was not.

With three small kids under four, I was thankful that my amazing niece Lindsay was willing to fly back from Michigan to California and help care for us all. I was out of commission for about eight weeks, which was the worst. I could still hop on one foot and got myself an ultra-cool scooter that I could race awkwardly, but I had three littles who had suddenly been endowed with super speed and I could not catch them. Having my mobility suspended was definitely challenging. It was hard to ask for help. It was hard to adjust to a different rhythm. It was hard to take the time to heal.

I can't even imagine what it was like for that man Peter and John encountered, who had been crippled from birth and needed people to carry him wherever he went. He was utterly dependent on others to move anywhere. I can only imagine that he often felt unseen, unappreciated, and unloved. But Jesus saw him. Peter and John saw him. They did not pass him by but looked right at him and healed him.

In this lesson, we will continue with the aftermath of what we read yesterday in Acts 3. Peter and John were able to heal the crippled man by the Beautiful Gate to the temple court's entrance. A large crowd gathered in awe and wonder, which was the perfect opportunity for Peter to teach them about the resurrected Jesus.

Jesus was no longer in their presence, but He was not dead. He was alive. His power and kindness were unmatched and still poured out on Jerusalem's people through His disciples. Peter and John stepped forward with boldness, courage, and gusto. Memories about Peter's retreat and denial when Jesus was arrested were long gone. He had been filled and emboldened with the Holy Spirit to stand up in the face of adversity. Jesus was building His church upon this rock, Simon Peter.

Read Acts 4:1-4. Who came over to Peter and John while speaking with the people?

How were they feeling? Why?

What did they do to Peter and John?

The temple was not just for religious gatherings but was also a place for teaching, socializing, and public interaction. After Peter and John healed the crippled beggar, a crowd gathered around Solomon's Colonnade (Acts 3:11).[1]

Solomon's Colonnade was located on the eastern side of the temple's outer court. A series of layers made up the structure of the temple. The outer layer was the Gentile court, where anyone was permitted. Then, there was another layer called the Outer Court or Women's Court, where only Jews were permitted. Both Jewish men and women were permitted in this section. Solomon's Colonnade, or Solomon's Porch, was located along this eastern wall and was named after Israel's King Solomon. It was often used as a gathering area for intellectual discussion, teaching, and debate.

The Jewish historian Josephus describes Solomon's Porch this way:

> There was a porch without the temple, overlooking a deep valley, supported by walls of four hundred cubits, made of four square stones, very white; the length of each stone was twenty cubits, and the breadth six; the work of king Solomon, who first founded the whole temple.[2]

Model of Jerusalem Temple

The priests who came over to Peter and John were the ones on duty that day. Priests were part of the tribe of Levi, one of the twelve tribes of Israel. Not everyone from the Levite tribe was a priest, but those who qualified (physical and age qualifications) as priests would always come from this tribe. Their job was to care for the temple and offer sacrifices on behalf of the people. They had to remain ceremonially clean to perform their duties before a holy God. By the time of Jesus's ministry, the Jewish priesthood held a lot of political and spiritual power.[3]

Following the resurrection of Jesus, believers lived under a new covenant where no priest was needed as a mediator between God and humans, then or now. Jesus serves as that mediator bridge.

Look up 1 Peter 2:9.

We don't have a lot of historical records about what the captain of the temple guard did, but in one historical reference, he is said to have been responsible for twenty-four guards who were stationed around the temple courts and was second-in-command to the high priest.[4]

The Sadducees were a group of upper-class, wealthy Jewish men who had specific views about the teachings of the Torah. In particular, they did not believe in the resurrection of the dead. They believed there was no afterlife, no spiritual realm, and no angels.

The message that Peter and John were preaching to the people got the Sadducees all riled up because Peter and John preached a resurrected Jesus

(Acts 3:15). The Sadducees's influence likely won the day in this gathering; they had Peter and John put in jail overnight.

Let's do some math.

- At Pentecost, three thousand men came to believe (Acts 2:41).
- Luke wrote in Acts that after this encounter, the number of men who were believers was now five thousand (Acts 4:4).

How many men came to believe in Jesus through this despite it ending in an uproar?

Read Acts 4:5-7.

The leaders called a meeting. It was the Supreme Court of the temple. The three groups of the Sanhedrin in their high court were the rulers, elders, and teachers. Annas was the high priest from AD 6–15 and was removed by the Romans. He was succeeded by his son Eleazar and then his son-in-law, Caiaphas. Caiaphas was high priest when Jesus was put on trial and sentenced to death. The Jews still recognized Annas as high priest (Luke 3:2; John 18:13, 24). We don't know who John or Alexander were, but they were part of the interrogation of Peter and John.[5] They wanted to know how in the world these two men could heal a crippled man at the temple.

Read Acts 4:8-12. What was Peter filled with as he answered these high-ranking men of office?

How did Peter describe this miracle?

To whom did Peter give credit for the power to heal the crippled man?

Write out Acts 4:12.

Take a minute to stop and worship with Hillsong Worship and sing "What A Beautiful Name."

Circle what was found. Write the name that Peter described in BIG LETTERS here:

Oh, yes. The precious, powerful, beautiful name of Jesus. A miracle that began at the Beautiful Gate was all about the beautiful Savior whom Peter passionately proclaimed.

Can you think of a time when calling upon the name of Jesus was powerful enough in your life to transform a moment of fear, anxiety, or weakness?

Read Acts 4:13-22. What did the Sanhedrin see in Peter and John?

What did they note about their education, status in society, and whom they hung out with?

What (or rather who) was the evidence standing next to Peter and John?

I wonder if the healed man was standing still the whole time…I imagine him getting his running man dance moves on. Stretching, bending, an occasional leap. Ya know, just for a little reminder to those around him of *what just happened.*

Look at Acts 3:2 and Acts 4:22. How long had that man been unable to walk, stand, run, leap, and dance?

The number forty has a special significance in the Bible.

- God flooded the earth for forty days and nights—then the Lord gave a rainbow.
- Moses fasted for forty days and nights—then the Lord gave the Ten Commandments.
- The Israelites wandered for forty years in the desert—then the Lord gave them the Promised Land.
- Jesus fasted in solitude for forty days and nights—then He began His public ministry.
- Jesus ascended into heaven forty days after the crucifixion, commissioning the disciples.

Forty signifies transformation. There is new life, new significance, new growth.

The Sanhedrin had a little chat and decided that all of Jerusalem had heard what had happened. To their shock and disappointment, they were discovering that the name of Jesus had not gone away with the Crucifixion. They thought they were done with Him. To their surprise and wonder, even the mere mention of *the name of Jesus* was filled with power. They had to shut that down.

In Acts 4:18, what did they command of Peter and John?

Summarize how Peter and John answered them in Acts 4:19 -20.

Sometimes, choosing to obey God is a hard choice with repercussions.

According to recent research by Open Doors International, almost 340 million Christians around the world live in countries where they suffer from some sort of persecution. That is one out of every seven people. These persecuted brothers and sisters in Christ face arbitrary arrest, violence, and a full range of human rights violations, and they are even killed for their faith.[6] Thankfully, Peter and John were allowed to go in this situation. But they had been willing to obey God even unto death.

What does Jesus say that true discipleship is? Write out Matthew 16:24.

What are the three things that Jesus says we must do:

1.

2.

3.

Write in your own words what those three things mean.

1.

2.

3.

Write a prayer of commitment to Jesus below. How far are you willing to go to take a stand for what God says over the authorities of this world? Where are tensions running high for Christians in our world? Where do you want to cast the authority of Jesus? Pray for the authorities in this world.

Sometimes, choosing to obey God is a hard choice with repercussions.

Try filling in the blanks to help you learn the verse.

His _____ power has given us _____ we _____
for a godly _____ through our _____ of him who
_____ us by his own _____ and _____.

(2 Peter 1:3)

DAY 3: HOOKED ON POSSIBILITY

Teaching my four kids to water-ski has been so much fun. I would get in the water with them, and my husband would usually drive the boat. I'd help them get the rope set between their skis, make sure the skis were tight on their feet, and help them crouch in the water, ready to pop up. I'd balance them as long as I could when the boat revved, the rope went taught, and the moment of truth came.

What a glorious day when each one was able to pop up, hold on for dear life, and experience the thrill of skimming over the water. I was the maniac mom left at the sandbar, cheering wildly for the victory. Sometimes, I could even rally complete strangers in surrounding boats to share the joy of the moment, and everyone out on the water would join in clapping and cheering for the newly christened water-skier.

Speaking of adrenaline, as we step back into the story with Peter and John, theirs must have been pumping strong. They had seen God perform a beautiful miracle, got to preach, enlivened by the power of the Holy Spirit, were arrested, thrown in jail, and released. But God was with them, and even though they were in the hot seat with the Sanhedrin, they did not quit. Our boys, Peter and John, were utterly outnumbered and outranked. The heat of shame radiates off the page as we hear the humiliation, embarrassment, and anger of the Sanhedrin. The leaders in Jerusalem were outraged and wanted Peter and John to get out. Let's see what they did.

Read Acts 4:21-22. What two things does Acts 4:21 say that the Sanhedrin did to Peter and John after hearing them defy their orders not to speak or teach in the name of Jesus?

_____ Threaten them   _____ Let them go   _____ Hide them

_____ Imprison them   _____ Stone them   _____ Beat them

What does Acts 4:21 say about why they did this?

Peter and John were released with some threats and returned to the other believers to report all that happened. Instead of being frightened or going into hiding, they did something remarkable. They asked for **more**.

Read Acts 4:23-24. Where did Peter and John go after they were released?

Can you imagine the group leaning in, listening with awe and delight about the miracle of the healing of the crippled man, their eyes growing wide and holding their breath when Peter and John told them about being thrown in jail?

What was their collective response after hearing what Peter and John had just been through?

As a group, the believers were in this together with Peter and John. Overflowing with thanksgiving, they were compelled to pray together. There was a Christ-centered unity that God should be exalted and thanked at that moment.

How is the experience of praying in a group different for you than praying alone?

As we read the prayer of Acts 4:24-30, let's see what we can learn about prayer from them. God always hears our prayers and encourages us to pray. Often, I have found that reading the prayers of others can encourage my own prayer life. They provide examples of how others have prayed. I especially love the prayers in the Bible because prayer can span across the centuries and still

God always hears our prayers and encourages us to pray.

unite the hearts of believers. I find that remarkable, mysterious, and beautiful all rolled up in one.

In Acts 4:24, how did they begin their prayer and address God?

Sovereign means the one who holds ultimate or supreme power. Even the way that they opened their prayer showed their deep reliance, faith, and hopeful expectation.

Look up these verses. What do they all have in common?

- Psalm 71:5
- Psalm 73:28
- Psalm 140:7
- Psalm 71:16
- Psalm 109:21

After the authors of these psalms name and exalt God, they recognize what He made. List the four things that they credit God with making.

1.

2.

3.

4.

As you read the next part of Peter and John's prayer in Acts 4:25-26, you'll notice that they recognize the Holy Spirit was speaking through the mouth of whom?

Look up Psalm 2:1-2. What do you notice?

In their prayer, Peter and John quoted King David, who wrote much of the Psalms. David was known as a man after God's own heart (v. 22). He was not perfect and made plenty of mistakes. But he always returned to his faith.

Peter and John knew much of the Old Testament because of the importance of oral tradition in the Jewish faith and culture, even though they were not considered "educated." The Scriptures were recited in the synagogue and passed down from generation to generation. As Peter and John thought about what had just happened to them, this passage of Scripture probably came to mind.

In Acts 4:27, who do they list as conspiring?

1.

2.

3.

4.

Who did they plot against?

How did they describe Jesus?

In Acts 4:28, John and Peter recognized two major things that God provides. What were they?

1.

2.

Let's spend a little bit of time here considering these two things. Often, I think about and ask God for His will and power. How about you? These two things feel heavy, important, and sometimes veiled from our understanding. The knowledge that God provides us with access to understand and know His *will* and *power* is comforting, thrilling, and a little overwhelming. How do we access these things, and what do we do with them?

Write out Revelation 4:11.

God's *will* and His *power.*

Sometimes, we read a verse like Acts 4:28 and can end up scratching our heads. Does God decide beforehand everything that should happen? Are we puppets? Do we have free will? How does that work with a statement like this?

Yes, God knows all things.

*If our hearts condemn us, we know that God is greater than our hearts, **and he knows everything**.*

(1 John 3:20, emphasis added)

But, yes, we have free will.

No temptation has overtaken you except what is common to mankind. And God is faithful; he will not let you be tempted beyond what you can bear. But when you are tempted, he will also provide a way out so that you can endure it.

(1 Corinthians 10:13)

So which is it? Is God orchestrating all our decisions, or do we get to make decisions? If God knows everything, why does He allow my pain? Why does He allow bad things to happen all around us, things that are unfair, unjust, and downright evil?

It's hard to wrap our heads around both ideas. Often, people like to believe that we deserve what we get. If we are successful, it's because we are good. If we are unsuccessful, it is because we are bad. But this is not good theology.[1] Life is hard for everyone. Every person suffers in some way.

Hard looks different for each person, but it is a reality for all because we all live in a broken world. Sin entered the life of every human after Adam and Eve had the free will to disobey God. Free will is a gift because it means we are free to choose God and we are free to disobey God. Each choice leads to consequences and either brings us closer to or further away from God. God does not use His power to control everything we do. A relationship of trust and care means much more when given freely rather than by force.

God does not want bad things to happen to us, but the reality of our world is that bad things are all around us because of sin.[2] Sin brought every form of brokenness, hurt, pain, and evil into our world. We live in it, around it, and sometimes get deeply impacted by it.

Jesus showed us that God does not always prevent bad things from happening. Jesus Himself had to endure the pain and humiliation of a trial, severe whipping, exposure, mockery, slaps, beatings, and the painful death of crucifixion. Trials come to all of us, but God is there with us and for us when bad things happen. God suffers alongside us when we suffer. God gives us strength. God gives us hope. God gives us our next steps.

Trials come to all of us, but God is there with us and for us when bad things happen. God suffers alongside us when we suffer. God gives us strength. God gives us hope. God gives us our next steps.

Peter and John were leaning into both God's power and God's will for their ministry and what had just happened with their imprisonment and verbal beating.

Read Acts 4:29. What did they ask God for?

Read these passages about boldness:
- Proverbs 28:1
- Mark 15:43
- Acts 13:46
- Romans 10:20
- 2 Corinthians 3:12

Which one impacts your heart the most today? Why?

Lord, make us bold like Peter. Where do you need some boldness in your life?

Read Acts 4:30. What did they ask God to do? By whose authority?

Peter and John asked God to continue to work through them, in spite of the imprisonment, threats, and hardship. They wanted boldness to continue to heal and perform signs and wonders by the name of Jesus—the very name they were just told not to utter. There was no stopping them. They were filled with the Spirit of God and emboldened to do hard things no matter what was to come.

What a prayer. What faith. I want me some of that. Lord, make me bold. Speak your word through me with **great boldness**. Pour out your Spirit and make yourself known in our world through your miraculous deeds.

In the word of the prophet Habakkuk:

Lord, I have heard of your fame;
  I stand in awe of your deeds, Lord.
Repeat them in our day,
  in our time make them known;
  in wrath remember mercy.
    (Habakkuk 3:2, emphasis added)

Read Acts 4:31. What happened after they prayed? What were they all filled with?

How did they continue to proclaim the message of Jesus to those around them?

Whew. Hooked on possibility. I love it. I'm feeling emboldened by their faith, prayer, commitment, mindset, and heart. Let's do it...

Who is ready to play for TEAM JESUS? Write a big YES if you are in.

WEEK 5 FOCUS VERSE: LEARN IT AND LIVE IT.

Try filling in the blanks to help you learn the verse.

His _____ power has given us _____ we _____ for a godly _____ through our _____ of him who _____ us by his own _____ and _____.

(2 Peter 1:3)

DAY 4: TIDES OF RESILIENCE

Make new friends, but keep the old;
One is silver and the other gold.

Did anyone else sing that in Brownies? We all herded around town in our brown uniforms, singing songs and earning badges like there was no tomorrow. Eventually, I graduated to become a cookie-prenuer with the Girl Scouts. We moved from one flattering color to another. Who chose those colors, anyway? Those green uniforms could not be missed. We worked fervently to fill our sashes with patches...especially during cookie sales.

Thin Mints. Need I say more?

Maybe we should just pause here because I know you are thinking of your favorite flavor Girl Scout cookie. What is it? Write it here. I even have a verse to let you meditate on its goodness for a moment.

Taste and see that the LORD *is good.*
        (Psalm 34:8)

Fun times. We had meetings and even did a few field trips. Since I went to a public school, it was my earliest experience with uniforms until I started playing sports. Uniforms helped unify us, so that we could see one another as part of the same group, the same team, with a unified mission and goal.

In this lesson, we continue our adventures with Peter and see how the Holy Spirit unified the early believers in some powerful ways.

In Acts 4:32, what does it say that the believers all shared? There are two things to look for that they shared internally in their community and two they shared externally with people in society around them.[1] See if you can find them.

Internal

1.

2.

External

1.

2.

Our internal motivations are sometimes even harder to share than our external ones. I've been in church leadership for more than twenty years and getting a group of believers to be unified is no easy task. Especially during political seasons. Aye yi yi.

These believers did not abandon their homes (Acts 2:46; 12:12) and start a colony; rather, they believed all they had belonged to one another. They were compelled to look out for one another and share what they had with those in need.[2]

This passage is special because not only were the new believers getting along but so were the disciples. They had come a long way from walking with Jesus and debating with one another.

Do you remember how difficult it was for the disciples to get along?

Read Luke 9:46-47 and Luke 22:24-27. About what did the disciples argue?

Acts 4:32 emphasizes unity as the primary catalyst for seeing a remarkable community form.

Write out Acts 4:33 and circle the word *power* every time it is used in the verse.

What does power mean about how God works differently from this world?

What were the *apostles* preaching about?

Were the apostles the same people as the disciples? Good question. I'm glad you asked.

Disciple language was used when Jesus was here on earth since a disciple followed the teachings of a rabbi. Disciples were students or learners. Any follower of Jesus devoted to learning from Him was considered a disciple. There were twelve disciples that Jesus specifically called, but many others were disciples of Jesus.

An apostle is someone who is a messenger or sent by God. In Acts, the term "apostles" primarily applied to those who had met and followed Jesus during his life. After Jesus's ascension into heaven, they continued to spread the teachings of Jesus and the powerful message of His death and resurrection for the forgiveness of our sins.[3]

What was powerfully at work in the apostles?

Read Acts 4:34-37. What stands out to you as being remarkable about this group of people who believed in Jesus?

Why do you think it is different today?

How did the believers with extra resources give a house, land, or money to the apostles?

In New Testament times, to lay something at one's feet indicated that you trusted him or her and were yielding to his or her authority. This was a custom of respect. The believers trusted what God was doing through the apostles. Trusting the apostles showed the community's faith in the message, proclaiming that Jesus was the promised Messiah. This trust was a factor that helped build and grow the early church. Those who had resources gave generously so that everyone's needs were met.

As we read the next passage of Scripture, remember what you just read about the generous environment the believers had created. It was radical. They lived out a remarkable culture of care, unity, and collaborative compassion. It is beautiful to think about and still leaves me in awe at the transformative work of the Holy Spirit in the hearts and minds of those early believers. They were all in with their lives, their trust, and their possessions. Just when things were dialed in and there was a sweet momentum, Satan tried to sneak in and rob this community of the joy and kindness they were experiencing.

Read Acts 5:1-2. What were the names of the husband-and-wife couple in Acts 5:1?

Who knew about the decision to split the money?

Read Acts 5:3-4.

Peter was rightly upset about what Ananias did, but the response seemed harsh, didn't it? After all, Ananias gave half the money to the church. Wasn't that still generous, even if it wasn't all the proceeds? Why in the world was this such a huge issue, causing Peter to speak and act so harshly toward Ananias?

Sometimes, people use this passage to say that Christians were required to give all their possessions or land to the church. But that is not true. Peter even told Ananias that he could have kept the money.[4]

It wasn't about the money.

The emphasis here was a heart issue. Ananias was trying to make himself and Sapphira look just as generous as Barnabas and the others who really did give everything to the church openly and honestly. Instead, they tried to deceive the church. Satan was the original deceiver. He whispered lies that looked like half-truths. God never wanted his people to be good at deception.

> "'Do not steal.'
> "'Do not lie.'
> "'Do not deceive one another.'"
> *(Leviticus 19:11)*

From the very beginning, God has called Satan a liar.

From the very beginning, God has called Satan a liar.

Read Revelation 12:9. What does it say that Satan does to the whole world?

Read John 8:44. How did Jesus describe Satan?

In this event in Acts, the problem with Ananias and Sapphira giving only half the income was deception—presenting the money as if it were *all* they had. They brought a false narrative and tried to pass off their deception as full generosity to the community. Ananias and Sapphira wanted the benefits of being seen the same as Barnabas and other generous givers without giving the entire sale amount. This was the beginning of Satan's infiltration into the community of believers.[5] The early church was growing and strong, but it was still full of sinful people. Pride and greed are strong temptations, and Satan knew how to whisper in Ananias's and Sapphira's ears to tempt them.

In Acts 5:3-4, who are the three names Peter says that Ananias lied to?

1.

2.

3.

Write out John 14:6.

Why do you think lying to God, especially when you are representing yourself to others as a follower of Jesus, grieves the heart of God so deeply?

Read Acts 5:5-6. What happened to Ananias?

Read Acts 5:7-10. How long had passed before Sapphira came to the group?

Did Peter give her the chance to speak truthfully?

_____ Yes _____ No

How did Sapphira respond?

_____ Same story as Ananias.

_____ She said she didn't know anything about it.

_____ She said they needed some of the money for their bills.

_____ She said she forgot.

What did Peter directly accuse her of doing in Acts 5:9?

When Jesus was tempted three times by Satan in the wilderness, He gave Satan an interesting response.

Write out Matthew 4:7.

Peter knew that Ananias and Sapphira conspired in advance, were deceived by Satan, and had agreed to test the Spirit of the Lord. They were trying to pull one over on God. But God sees. God knows. God hears. You can't expect to sneak around God. He is above all things and knows all things.

Unfortunately, this account ended in a doubly sad event. Both Ananias and Sapphira died. Not only were their deaths tragic but look at what this did to the community.

Read Acts 5:11. What was the community filled with after they experienced this?

Um. Yes. I think I would be scared too if I witnessed this firsthand. Even reading about it puts the fear in me. It was a very real battle of the will and a spiritual battle with the Holy Spirit. It was a battle with Satan, and Satan would not win the day. Jesus had already defeated him with the Resurrection. Not today, Satan.

Take a few minutes to list any greed or pride in your heart today. Ask God to help you turn it into honest generosity and humility so that God can use you to help build up the body of Christ:

Take a moment to sing "Run Devil Run" with Crowder and proclaim this victory chant over Satan.

Ask God to make you bold in your soul to confront the lies of Satan.

Draw a picture of soul courage in the tides of resistance.

WEEK 5 FOCUS VERSE: LEARN IT AND LIVE IT.

Try filling in the blanks to help you learn the verse.

His _____ power has given us _____ we _____

for a godly _____ through our _____ of him who

_____ us by his own _____ and _____.

(2 Peter 1:3)

DAY 5: DEPTHS OF FORTITUDE

Have you ever seen something that you couldn't believe? I remember watching my dad do a magic trick when I was a kid. He was seemingly able to pound cards right through our dining room table. I was in awe. Eventually, I learned how he did the trick—it was only a sleight-of-hand illusion to make it look like magic.

That is why Jesus is a kazillion times more amazing than any "magic" trick. He didn't try to fool people. He really did acts of healing. He did the miraculous. He was fully human but also fully God. The laws of physics, the laws of nature, and the laws of gravity did not apply to Him.

In this lesson, we will continue to see Peter and the apostles show up, no matter what, to proclaim Jesus to everyone around them.

Read Acts 5:12. What did the apostles perform?

1.

2.

Read these passages in Scripture. Be alert for the same two things that are mentioned.

- Exodus 7:3
- Jeremiah 32:20
- Daniel 6:27
- Matthew 24:24
- John 4:48
- Acts 6:8
- Acts 14:3

What did you discover in these verses?

No single word in Scripture is used for the word *miracle*. Our English word *miracle* comes from a Latin word, *miraculum*, which means "something that causes wonder."[1]

Four Greek words are most often translated "miracle":

1. Ἔργον (*ergon*)—works or deeds
2. Δύναμις (*dunamis*)—powers
3. Σημεῖον (*semeion*)—signs
4. Τέρας (*teras*)—wonders[2]

They are each used to explain amazing events. The biblical writers used these words to talk about exceptional actions that God was doing in the world. They were spiritual realities that did not conform to the laws of nature.

What were the two emotions people felt toward the apostles, according to Acts 5:3?

1.

2.

No one else dared to join them. Even though people were in awe and respected them, there was fear. Others were not courageous enough to align themselves with the apostles' actions.[3] Despite this, Scripture says that more and more people came to faith and believed in Jesus.

Read Acts 5:13-15. Who did the people bring to Peter?

1.

2.

Where did they put these people who needed the touch of God to heal them? Circle the one that Acts 5:15 describes:

On donkeys   On the grass   On the streets

On the mountain   In Peter's boat

Long before Wendy offered to sew on Peter Pan's famous lost shadow, God was working through the apostle Peter's shadow in a mighty way.

What happened to the people who encountered Peter's shadow?

This is similar to the encounter a woman had with Jesus. Read Luke 8:43-48. How was she healed?

Read the prophecy of Zechariah in Luke 1:76-79. As you read these verses, pay special attention to Luke 1:79.

This song is a prophecy about the one who is to come, for whom John the Baptist would prepare the way. John the Baptist was the cousin of Jesus, miraculously given to Elizabeth and Zechariah in their advanced age.

What is the promise in that verse?

Who do you think lives in darkness and the shadow of death?

When have you lived in the shadows or experienced darkness?

Shadows are only a partial representation of who we are. The sun has to shine on us at the right angle for a shadow to be cast on the ground. Peter had the SON of God Almighty shining not only on him but through him. The presence of God was so powerful that even when Peter walked down the street, God used him to heal.[4] Just being in the vicinity of the presence of God is enough to receive healing when we have faith that Jesus is real, that He is who He says He is, and that He has the power to transform brokenness into beauty.

> *How priceless is your unfailing love, O God!*
> *People **take refuge in the shadow of your wings.***
> *(Psalm 36:7, emphasis added)*

> *When all the people were being baptized, Jesus was baptized too. And as he was praying, heaven was opened and **the Holy Spirit descended on him in bodily form like a dove.** And a voice came from heaven: "You are my Son, whom I love; with you I am well pleased."*
> *(Luke 3:21-22, emphasis added)*

Where do you need to take refuge today in the shadow of the wings of the Almighty?

Read Acts 5:17-20. What happened to Peter and the other apostles?

Who rescued them? What did their rescuer tell them to do?

Let's finish up our journey with Peter in this section. Peter and the apostles were miraculously released from jail by one of God's angels.

Read Acts 5:21-32 to see how those around them reacted.

Why were the Sanhedrin so upset?

This had to be very confusing for the Sanhedrin. Not only were the apostles ignoring their mandates, but the people were supporting the work and teaching of the apostles rather than the Sanhedrin. This was like a slap in the face to their authority. They were furious at losing their influence. How embarrassing for them to have their jailed captives escape with no one knowing how it happened. Can you imagine if they had digital cameras to record the escape back then?

Peter continued to respond as he had before. Write out what Peter said in Acts 5:29.

God Jesus

GOD EXALTED HIM TO HIS OWN RIGHT HAND AS PRINCE AND SAVIOR THAT HE ➡ Jesus MIGHT BRING ISRAEL TO REPENTANCE AND FORGIVE THEIR SINS. ACTS 5:31

Acts 5:31 is a very clarifying verse. It gets to the heart of Peter and the other apostles' message.

Read Isaiah 9:6. In this prophecy, what are the four titles given to the child to be born?

_____

_____

_____

_____

How does the Prince of Peace bring peace when we feel forgiven? How can this help fight anxiety in our lives today?

Read Acts 5:33-42.

In this section, God rescued the apostles from death by using the words of Gamaliel, an esteemed Jewish teacher of the law. He was also the apostle Paul's teacher (Acts 22:3). Interestingly, the Talmud, which is a collection of ancient teachings for Jewish life, names Gamaliel as נָשִׂיא Nāśî', which means "prince," referring to him being the prince or leader of the Sanhedrin. Luke, our writer, made an interesting play on words and meaning with prince and high authority in these passages.[5]

Gamaliel persuaded the Sanhedrin with this speech:

*"Leave these men alone! Let them go! For if their purpose or activity is of human origin, it will fail. **But if it is from God,** you will not be able to stop these men; you will only find yourselves fighting against God."*

(Acts 5:38-39, emphasis added)

It is unclear if Gamaliel believed them. But Gamaliel did recognize that martyrdom usually does the opposite of what those who want someone dead intend. Rather than getting rid of the problem, it adds fuel to the fire.

The Sanhedrin was convinced but did not let the apostles go until they flogged them. Remember, Jesus was flogged before the Crucifixion. It was a horrible punishment. Jewish law allowed up to forty lashes with a leather whip.

It was considered that after forty, a person could die, so often only thirty-nine lashes were given so as not to accidentally exceed the prescribed amount. One-third of the lashes were given on the chest, and the other two-thirds were given on the back. The person lashing would stand on a stone above the offender, who stood in a bowed position. The blows would be accompanied by the recitation of admonishments from Scripture.[6]

The disciples were warned not to speak the name of Jesus again. It didn't work. *They never stopped.* Talk about depths of fortitude.

> Write a proclamation of commitment to standing strong and speaking faithfully about Jesus that is true for you.

Worship with Katy Nichole and sing "In Jesus Name (God of Possible)."

WEEK 5 FOCUS VERSE: LEARN IT AND LIVE IT.

Try filling in the blanks to help you learn the verse.

His _____ power has given us _____ we _____

for a godly _____ through our _____ of him who

_____ us by his own _____ and _____.

(2 Peter 1:3)

Video Viewer Guide: *Week 5*

Jesus was _____.

This Holy Spirit was given to _____ believer _____.

At this Festival of the Harvest, a _____ _____ had begun.

But now, there was a new fruit that would nourish lives
at a _____ level.

When we are called into a season of _____,
God is still _____.

When things are unclear, _____ in community.

Prayer is not just about _____; it's about _____.

Stay _____ to the responsibilities
that God has given you.

Discussion Questions: *Week 5*

Think about these questions as you prepare to meet with your small group.

- Who are some of the people in your life who have been spiritually influential?

- What is one of your favorite podcasts, books, apps, or other spiritual resources?

- What stands out to you about the account of Peter at Pentecost?

- In what ways would you like to invite the Holy Spirit to be active in your life?

- What is one thing that you would like your group to pray for you this week?

specific kindness

Write down how you can encourage someone in your small group this week. When will you pray for them? When will you text them?

Hey Friend!

I just wanted to let you know that I admire these specific traits that I see in your life…

Thank you for representing them well to me and the body of Christ!

Perfectly FLAWED and FAITHFUL

(Peter Persisted for Jesus)

FOCUS Verse

Each of you should use whatever gift you have received to serve others, as faithful stewards of God's grace in its various forms.

(1 Peter 4:10)

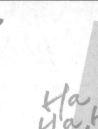

TAKE ACTION

Make a list of the people to whom you want to remain faithful. What are three ways you can do that?

Serve
At your church.

FAITHFUL

Creation Corner

Plan to watch a sunrise or sunset. Enjoy the beauty of the colors God paints across the sky. What splendor that takes our breath away! It is as if heaven throws out a little joy in living color. Amid a broken world, consider how every sunrise and sunset shout about the hope Jesus extends abundantly. Read Psalm 65:8.

CREATE

Create some custom glass magnets. Cut round circles out of craft paper the size of flat round glass marbles (you can find at a dollar store in the craft section). Using Mod Podge, attach the circles to the bottom of the glass and then glue on a round magnet.

A Word from Peter

For fishermen, the anchor held us steady. It stopped us from drifting and held us secure during stormy conditions. As a fisherman who navigated the waters of the Galilee almost every day, I had long relied upon anchors to steady my boat amid the ebb and flow of the waves. With each descent into the depths, the anchor served as my steadfast companion, ensuring that I remained grounded in the fast-moving currents and waves that tried to push me off course. Yet it was not until I encountered Jesus, the carpenter from Nazareth, that I truly grasped the profound symbolism of the anchor.

The anchor means steadfastness. It was my boat's tether to the depths of the sea. I came to see Jesus as the anchor of my soul. He grounded me through the storms of life and held me steady in the face of adversity. Just as an anchor provided stability amid turmoil, so too did my faith in Jesus anchor my soul. It offered me hope and assurance in the midst of life's tempests. Though the winds howled and the waves crashed, I found solace in knowing that I was securely held by the unbreakable bond of Christ's love, forever anchored in the depths of His grace.

We have this hope as an anchor for the soul, firm and secure.
(Hebrews 6:19)

Shalom,

Simon Peter

DAY 1: IN THE SAME BOAT

One of the reasons I loved moving to Southern California to go to grad school was the diversity. I love the eclectic mix of people that Los Angeles represents. It means really good restaurants serving every kind of food imaginable. Museums that display incredible cultural heritage and art. Multiple languages heard when just walking down the street. All forms of music are played. The different backgrounds and cultures can sometimes bump into one another but seeing God's abundant creativity can take my breath away. If only it could always inspire people to be more creative rather than allow the focus to become centered around differences.

Racial tensions plague our country, our world, and our cities. These tensions impact our hearts and lives. Sometimes, our struggle to treat people equally stems from our childhood influences, the ideas we were taught in school, or even the music, movies, books, and culture we surround ourselves with today.

Fighting racism is important to the heart of God. Want to know how I know that? The story we will read in Scripture today is powerful for many reasons, but one is what God revealed to Peter. The way things have always been is not how they need to stay. In God's kingdom, diversity and unity can coexist through the bond of Jesus. When unity amid diversity happens, it is surprising. It's radical. It's powerful. And it is beautiful.

In God's kingdom, diversity and unity can coexist through the bond of Jesus.

What are some of the challenges with racism that you have experienced in your own life?

What are some relationships that have helped you in a positive way to challenge stereotypes and culture?

Today, the church has the opportunity and the responsibility to live out what God started with Peter and Cornelius. Are you ready to meet Cornelius? Let's do it.

Read Acts 10:1-8.

What was Cornelius's profession?

How does Acts 10:2 describe Cornelius's family?

What time did Cornelius hear from God?
_____ 10:00 a.m.   _____ 12:00 p.m.   _____ 3:00 p.m.   _____ 7:00 p.m.

What happened?

_____ He had a vision.   _____ He had an argument.

_____ He went for a walk.   _____ He was arrested.

Who appeared to Cornelius in his vision?

Cornelius immediately knew this was from the Lord and asked, "What is it, Lord?"

What are the three things that the angel told Cornelius?

1.

2.

3.

Caesarea is currently called Caesarea-by-the-Sea (Maritima), distinguishing it from the other "Caesareas." When Cornelius, a Gentile who lived in Caesarea, sent his men to Joppa (modern-day Jaffa) to find the apostle Peter, they would have had to walk (or ride) for almost thirty-nine miles. An average walking pace would take about thirteen hours. By camel, it would take about six to eight hours.[1]

Caesarea Maritima was built by Herod the Great on the shores of the Mediterranean in honor of Caesar. This seaport city was strategically located and placed between significant trade routes. It was built like a contemporary Greco-Roman city and was laid out on a grid. After Herod's death, Caesarea became the new capital of the Roman province of Judea. When Jesus went to Jerusalem to celebrate the Passover, the province had a prefect (like a governor) who also traveled there to keep order. His name was Pontius Pilate.[2] Archaeological work in Caesarea has recently uncovered a stone that says, "Pontius Pilatus, of Judea," that provides archaeological evidence for what the Bible describes.

Read Acts 10:9-23 to discover what Peter was doing while Cornelius was in Caesarea.

As Peter approached Joppa, he paused on his journey and was hosted by Simon the tanner. A tanner would take animal skins and hides and turn them into leather. This was smelly work, so often tanners lived a distance away from the rest of the villagers.

What time did Peter stop to pray?

_____ 10:00 a.m.   _____ 12:00 p.m.   _____ 3:00 p.m.   _____ 7:00 p.m.

Where was Peter?

_____ On the road   _____ On a mountain

_____ On his boat   _____ On a roof

The Gospels and Acts refer to Jews praying at the third, sixth, and ninth hours, referring to about three hours after sunrise, noon, and three hours after noon. This would be 9:00 a.m., 12:00 p.m., and 3:00 p.m.

Peter was hungry and ready for some L-U-N-C-H. While the food was being prepared, Peter fell into a trance.

*Photos
(from left to right):*

Ancient ruins of Caesarea Maritima. Peter traveled from Joppa to visit Cornelius in his home in this city.

Me in Caesarea Maritima at the Pilate Stone.

King Herod's private palace villa ruins in Caesarea Maritima. This palace was one of ten—all with swimming pools .

Say what? I know. That is weird. What is a trance? What was happening? Well, the Greek word for "trance" is *ekstasis*, pronounced "ek'-stas-is."[3] Does that remind you of an English word? If you said "ecstasy," you are right. We get our word *ecstasy* from this Greek word. In the drug world, ecstasy is a hallucinogen that makes you see things that are not real. Unfortunately, that colors our approach to this word. But in biblical times, no narcotics framed the meaning of this word. It was used seven times in the New Testament to show a unique way that God communicated with people.

Thayer's Greek Lexicon describes a person in *ekstasis* as this: "although he is awake, his mind is drawn off from all surrounding objects and wholly fixed on things divine that he sees nothing but the forms and images lying within and thinks that he perceives with his bodily eyes and ears realities shown him by God."[4]

It may seem strange, but it was powerful. Peter fully knew that the things he saw were from God.

Write what Peter's vision was:

Peter was fully open with God about this. He was shocked. Horrified. Repelled by what he saw. How many times did God show Peter this same vision?

_____ 1   _____ 2   _____ 3   _____ 4

The number three is important in Scripture. It is often used to communicate wholeness or completeness. God repeated this message to Peter because it was so important, so different from what Peter had always known, and so that Peter would know it was from God.

Peter was trying to figure out what this disturbing vision meant when he was interrupted by the men that Cornelius had sent. Peter invited them in and was soon on his way with them.

Read Acts 10:23-29.

Peter had a nice entourage to travel with him. Some of the believers from Joppa went with him, the crew from Cornelius (remember, he was a Gentile), and the friends Peter was originally traveling with (Acts 10:9—don't forget the "they"). I wonder if Tabitha and Aeneas (see Acts 9:32-43) went along after God used Peter to heal them. I bet they did.

By the time Peter got to Cornelius's house and met all the people there, he had figured out something about the vision that God had given him. To understand it, let's get a little context.

Jews were anyone whose lineage could be traced back to one of the twelve tribes of Israel, who were from the twelve sons of Jacob. Gentiles were everyone else—basically anyone who was not Jewish. Jews and Gentiles had not interacted for centuries historically.

The differences between the two groups of people could be seen everywhere. They dressed differently, ate differently, washed differently, and worshipped differently. Their language, culture, schooling, and architecture were all different. One of the primary distinctions between Jews and Gentiles was the physical distinction of circumcision. This physical mark was a prominent feature that divided the two groups visibly. It was the outward mark of the eternal covenant between the Jewish people and God.[5]

God separated the Jews from the rest of the population to put a spotlight on how God's ways were different from the rest of the world. But now, the time had come for all people (both Jews and Gentiles) to have full access to God through Jesus and the Holy Spirit.

Read the prophecy from Joel 2:27-29 in the Old Testament. What did God promise?

Read Acts 10:30-48.

So good. So amazing. So powerful. Peter had grown so much in his faith that even when God called him to do something so contrary to his upbringing and tradition, he obeyed. Peter had moved from fear to powerful faith, and God showed up big time for him.

What happened in Acts 10:44 while Peter spoke and the crowd gathered in Cornelius's house was listening?

Let's get our worship on with "Good Grace" by Hillsong United.

Who was surprised by what happened in Acts 10:45?

What were the Gentile believers doing that was so surprising in Acts 10:46?

Peter ended up baptizing Gentiles. And the party was off and running. They were all in the same boat. Peter stayed with them for a few days, likely celebrating, encouraging, teaching, and beginning the first house church of Gentiles and Jews ever to exist. The CHURCH that Jesus described that Peter would have never imagined. For THIS, we have Jesus.

And I tell you that you are Peter, and on this rock, I will build my church, and the gates of Hades will not overcome it.

(Matthew 16:18)

Who would you be shocked to see in church one day? Make a list and pray for them right now. You just never know what Jesus will do through the power of the Holy Spirit.

Write a prayer asking Jesus to allow the gospel to penetrate their hearts and lives and the power of the Holy Spirit to be upon them in surprising ways.

WEEK 6 FOCUS VERSE: LEARN IT AND LIVE IT.

Our last verse for our last week. You can do it!

Each of _____ should use whatever _____ you have _____

to _____ others, as _____ _____ of God's

_____ in its _____ forms.

(1 Peter 4:10)

DAY 2: CATCH AND RELEASE

I love a good thunderstorm. Living in LA, we don't get many out here. But when I was growing up in Michigan, I loved to watch a storm begin to brew and move across our little lake. You could see it before it arrived. You could feel it. The air got ominous and everything got dark. Thunder and lightning would explode in the sky. You could feel the boom go all the way to your bones. When I was little, someone told me not to worry about the loud sound; God was just moving furniture around in heaven. But thunder definitely leaves an impression.

As did the Sons of Thunder (AKA James and John), who were like brothers to Peter and Andrew. They joined up with Jesus around the same time, fishermen turned surprising disciples of an itinerant, little-known rabbi. With awe and joy, they discovered Jesus was the Messiah they had prayed for their whole lives.

Those four men had likely known one another since childhood, splashing in the Galilee. Oh, the stories they could tell about one another. They could not believe that a rabbi like Jesus would invite their crew of rough-around-the-edges fishermen to join him. But He did.

And they did. All the way to the cross, the mind-blowing Resurrection, and His commissioning of the disciples to take the gospel to the ends of the earth. With the same passion that they threw one another into the sea and pulled in their nets, they preached the good news.

Read John 9:51-56. Why do you think Jesus gave James and John the nickname Βοανεργές (*Boanergés*), which means *sons of rage*?[1] Do you know anyone else like this?

Boanerges is an Aramaic term interpreted by Mark for his non-Jewish audience, who were probably Romans.[2] These men, who were dear friends of Peter, had also been with Jesus through it all. After Jesus ascended into heaven, they were enlivened with a courage they had never known.

Read Mark 16:19-20.

Filled with the very Spirit of God, they performed miracles, preached, healed, and pointed people to their friend and Savior—Jesus.

As we start our lesson today, let's do a recap. Peter had returned to Jerusalem with James and John for the Festival of Unleavened Bread. This was a Jewish holiday to remember the Passover. The Passover commemorates the night the Lord unleashed the tenth and final miracle in Egypt, during which every firstborn male would be struck down, including animals (Exodus 11:5). The Spirit of the Lord passed over the Hebrew households marked with blood over their doorposts (having been warned by God), and all the Israelites lived. However, because the Egyptians did not put the blood over their doorways, an untold number of firstborns perished. With great mourning and sorrow in his land, Pharaoh finally let the whole of the Hebrew nation go. The Jews were released from Egypt to go into the Promised Land of Israel.

The Feast of Unleavened Bread and the Passover reminded the people of this event every year. For this annual festival, the Passover would begin on the fourteenth day of the first month, and the Festival of Unleavened Bread would start on the fifteenth. For seven days, the Jews would eat bread made without any yeast. It was a pita party. Days one and seven would be days off from work, and they would gather as a people. Each day of that week a food offering would be given to the Lord.[3]

Peter, James, and John had celebrated the Feast of Unleavened Bread many times in their life. But this one would be different. Instead of celebration, there was horrific violence.

Read Acts 12:1-5. Who was in power? Who was he mad at? Who paid the price?

James lost his life and Peter was put in jail. I'm sure he wondered if his fate was to be the same as his dear friend James. Riddled with grief over losing James and the fear of his own death, Peter waited for his trial, and he waited upon God.

But the newly formed church, which knew the power of a resurrected Jesus, was praying for God to do what they knew He could do again: set the captive free!

Read Acts 12:6-11. How did Peter get out of prison?

a. A soldier let him out

b. Peter found a secret tunnel

c. The other disciples rescued him

d. An angel hit Peter and woke him up

Peter thought he was dreaming. He had no idea what was happening until the angel walked him to safety outside the city gate and up the street. Only then did God awaken Peter fully, and he became aware of his miraculous rescue.

What did Peter say in Acts 12:11 to indicate he knew who had rescued him?

Angels can bring messages from God, guide our actions, and rescue us from dangerous situations.

Have you or someone you know ever had an encounter with an angel? Describe it below:

> **Angels can bring messages from God, guide our actions, and rescue us from dangerous situations.**

Just remember, no matter what your encounter with an angel may have been, they are never the ones to be worshipped.[4] That is reserved for God alone. Read Revelation 22:8-9 to hear how an angel corrected John when he was tempted to bow down and worship an angel.

God must have needed to both protect and cause Peter to move quickly during this rescue. He likely put him in a dazed state to blindly follow the angel without doubt or question. I can only imagine that while sitting in that lonely, dark prison cell, Peter may have been overwhelmed with grief over his friend James's death, and the fear of what might await him as the same fate. But God had different plans! I love when God shows up in ways that we never expected.

Can you think of a time when God showed up for you in a way you never expected?

Read Acts 12:12-17.

This is an exciting description of what happened, but it can also get confusing because there are so many people named Mary in Scripture, as well as John and Mark. Let's untangle this a bit.

John Mark was a follower of Jesus who was first introduced to us in Acts. He was not one of the twelve disciples of Jesus, but he did join up with Paul and Barnabas on their missionary adventures (Acts 12:25). Tradition says John Mark was a disciple of Peter and is believed by many to have been the author of the Gospel of Mark.

This Scripture contains the only reference to this particular Mary. She was not Mary, the mother of Jesus, Mary Magdalene, or the sister of Martha, the three other well-known Marys in Scripture. This Mary must have had a larger home in Jerusalem since she had a servant who answered the door. Rhoda and Mary were believers and knew that Peter had been arrested.[5] When Peter appeared at their home, and Rhoda recognized his voice, she was so excited that she forgot to open the door. Instead, she rushed to tell the others, but no one believed her.

But faithful and exuberant Rhoda persisted that it was Peter. Go, Rhoda. Rhoda's name in Greek is παιδίσκη and means "rose." What a sweet aroma her courageous insistence was to the Lord despite no one listening to her.

Peter kept knocking.

Read Matthew 7:7-8. What does Jesus ask us to do when we desperately need the Lord's help?

Where do you need to keep knocking and asking Jesus to open the door for you?

When poor Peter was finally let in the house, everyone had to pick their jaws up off the floor. He was free. He was alive. He was with them. They must have had loud, joyous outcries of celebration because Peter immediately asked them to keep it down.

Can you imagine their faces and rapt attention as Peter described what had just happened?

He left a message to inform James and the other disciples about what happened, and he hightailed it out of there. Peter knew all the Jerusalem guards would be looking for him when they discovered his escape.

As Peter expected, the soldiers were confused, shocked, and frenzied to find Peter gone. King Herod was furious that someone interfered with his execution of Peter and ordered all the guards to be killed.

God had more plans for Peter and miraculously created a way for him to live another day. It was a catch and release like Peter had never experienced.

Write a prayer expressing your awe about God's ability to move miraculously. God is still doing miracles. Invite God to do one for you in your own life.

Let's get our worship on with Jesus Culture proclaiming "Freedom."

WEEK 6 FOCUS VERSE: LEARN IT AND LIVE IT.

Try filling in the blanks to help you learn the verse.

Each of _____ should use whatever _____ you have _____

to _____ others, as _____ _____ of God's

_____ in its _____ forms.

(1 Peter 4:10)

DAY 3: TANGLED LINES

Conflict is never easy. Sometimes we avoid it, hoping it will go away. Sometimes we have to deal with it head-on. When one of my dear friends started making some choices that were not honoring to God, it was hard to know what to do. Even after talking to her about it, she decided to continue with her choice. Our friendship shifted a bit. I still deeply cared about her but also knew that I had to be careful about the influence I let her have on my life when she no longer yielded to God's authority. It was so hard.

Have you ever lost a friend to conflict that you could not resolve?

Conflict followed the disciples wherever they went. In the next few chapters of Acts, the story's emphasis shifts from Peter to Paul. God transformed Paul, a man who had persecuted Christ-followers (Acts 9), with a dramatic encounter with Jesus on the road to Damascus. Just as Peter had dramatically changed his life from that of a fisherman to an evangelist, Paul became an impassioned preacher of the gospel of Jesus Christ.

Read Acts 9:15. Write down how God described Paul to a man named Ananias.

Paul was a Pharisee, a religious leader of the Jews. Pharisees were experts of the law and often were at odds with Jesus. The Pharisees regulated and enforced many of the Old Testament laws within the Jewish community. They put a huge amount of attention on the Jews' actions and outward behaviors that made them appear godly rather than on the motivation of their hearts. Jesus was frustrated by this and called them hypocrites in Matthew 23. Before Paul's conversion (when he was still called Saul), Paul was anti-Christian. He sought to imprison Christians who were known as members of "The Way."[1]

Read the following verses. What words are interesting to you in these passages?

- Read Isaiah 30:21   • Read Psalm 32:8   • Read Psalm 37:5

Write out John 14:6.

What words did Jesus use to describe Himself that were repeated from the Old Testament passages above?

Read Acts 9:20-25. How did people respond to Paul when they heard him preach about Jesus?

How did the Jews feel about Paul? What did they decide to do to Paul?

How did Paul escape?

Paul ran to Jerusalem, planning to join the disciples (including Peter). Read Acts 9:26. How did they respond?

Barnabas had to convince the disciples that Paul's conversion was real and that he could be trusted. The disciples were convinced and began to partner with Paul, but everywhere he went, the Jews were so angry at Paul that they kept trying to kill him (Act 9:29). The disciples sent Paul back to his hometown of Tarsus (Acts 9:11, 30), a province of Cilicia that is part of Turkey today. This was a great decision because tensions cooled in Jerusalem. With things less heated by Paul's presence, there was a time of peace, and the church was strengthened and grew (Acts 9:31).[2]

> Read Galatians 1:18. How long did Paul stay with Peter at the beginning of his call to ministry?

> Why do you think it was important for Paul and Peter to spend time together?

Acts 13–15 continues the story of how God used Paul to expand the church to the Gentiles—everyone else who was not Jewish. Since there was such tension between the Jews and Gentiles, Paul became God's unique leader in begining to build churches in Gentile communities.

Acts 16:37 tells us that Paul held Roman citizenship, which was greatly treasured because it offered protections others did not enjoy from the strong hand of Roman rule. A person could either be born into citizenship if their parents were Roman, or they could buy the privilege. Since Paul was born into a Jewish family in the city of Tarsus, he held citizenship since Tarsus was considered a "free city" by Rome, meaning it held local autonomy and (sometimes) tax-immunity privileges.[3]

In 42 BC, Tarsus, the Ivy League community of the ancient world, received special privileges from Gaius Julius Caesar Augustus, also known as Octavian. Augustus exempted the city from paying Roman taxes, and Tarsus grew as a prominent cultural and intellectual center. At some point, Paul's parents relocated him to Jerusalem to study Jewish laws under a very famous rabbi named Gamaliel (Acts 22:3).[4]

Paul went from Tarsus to many surrounding cities, proclaiming the truth of Jesus and planting churches wherever he was. When a hostile dispute about circumcision arose between groups, Paul and Barnabas returned to Jerusalem to check in with the believers there. Circumcision was a vital cultural and spiritual component of Judaism. The controversy centered on whether Gentiles (who were not circumcised) had to be circumcised to become followers of Jesus (who was Jewish).

Read Acts 15:6-21. Who stood up to address the assembly during this discussion? What event did he refer to that showed him that He accepted Gentiles as part of the family of God? (Hint: Acts 10:9-15)

In Acts 15:8, what did Peter say that God knows?

Read Luke 5:22. What does Jesus know?

How's your heart today? Take a moment to be honest with the Lord today with what is in your heart. No need to sugarcoat it; God sees our hearts.

- If your heart is feeling tired and weary, write out Psalm 51:10.
- If your heart is feeling hardened and cynical, write out Ezekiel 36:26.
- If your heart is feeling joyful and content, write out Psalm 28:7.

Read Acts 15:8. To whom did Peter say that God gave the Gentiles?

Does God distinguish between Jews and Gentiles now?
_____ Yes   _____ No   _____ Sometimes

Write out Galatians 3:28.

What does this verse say that Jesus can do?

_____ Unify us   _____ Confuse us

_____ Divide us   _____ Ignore us

How did Peter say that God purifies hearts? (Hint: Acts 15:9)

Read Luke 7:50. What saved this woman?

Read Romans 10:10. What saves us?

Read Ephesians 2:8. What is our part in faith?

Look up these verses about faith. Circle the one that speaks uniquely to you today.

• Hebrews 11:1 • 2 Corinthians 5:7 • Hebrews 11:6 • James 2:14

What did Peter tell this group of people who feuded over the issue of circumcision as he was trying to bring unity? Write out Acts 15:11.

Peter passed the mic to Paul and Barnabas, who began to tell stories of God's signs and wonders among the Gentiles. James, the leader and pastor of the church of Jerusalem, stood and told them not to make it difficult for Gentiles to become followers of Jesus (Acts 15:12-29).

Read 2 Peter 3:9. Whom does God want to be part of the family of God?

Read John 3:16. Whom does God love?

Read 1 Timothy 2:1-4. Whom does God want to save?

Peter, Paul, and the other leaders were working through some highly divisive issues in their church and culture. What were some of the key methods they used to work through the opposition to find a resolution?

What are some divisive issues in our church and culture today?

Read Acts 15:30-34. How would you summarize the reaction and response to the decision regarding this conflict?

Write out Acts 15:28.

What was not required of the Gentile believers? (Hint: Acts 15:5)

What was required of the Gentile believers?

1. _____ (food sacrificed to idols)

2. _____ (blood)

3. _____ (meat of strangled animals)

4. _____ (sexual immorality)

The death of Jesus on the cross also displayed the power of God. Jesus gave His life so that we could be forgiven of our wrongdoings (our sins) before God. There was power in His blood—the power to forgive, restore, and reunify us in a relationship with a holy, pure God.

Have you decided to let Jesus untangle your lines and forgive you, lead you, and invite you to follow Him just as Peter did? Write about this decision:

If you have never made that decision, today can be your day. You can use your own words and ask Jesus to forgive you and lead you from this day forward.

LEAD ON, King Jesus. Be my Good Shepherd. Be my leader, forgiver, and king of my life.

WEEK 6 FOCUS VERSE: LEARN IT AND LIVE IT.

Try filling in the blanks to help you learn the verse.

Each of _____ should use whatever _____ you have _____

to _____ others, as _____ _____ of God's

_____ in its _____ forms.

(1 Peter 4:10)

DAY 4: PARALLEL WATERS

My oldest daughter is learning to drive. It is such an exciting time—especially in the car. Brake. Brake. Brake More. Brake harder. Turn. Go. Stop. Whew. It's a workout. I hope I'm burning calories.

Actually, she is doing a great job. I remember learning to drive with the same passionate verbal exclamations from those teaching me. Learning involves correction, which means life involves allowing people we trust to speak into our lives.

In this lesson, a respected ministry leader of the early church offers some correction to another respected ministry leader. Put on your seat belt and join us for the bumpy ride.

Read Galatians 2:7. To whom was Paul asked to preach the gospel?

To whom was Peter asked to preach the gospel, according to Paul?

Read Galatians 2:8-10. Where was God at work?

Who did Paul name as pillars of the early church movement? (Hint: There are three.)

What did they extend to Paul and Barnabas?

In biblical times, the "right hand of fellowship" (v. 9) was a way to describe acceptance and inclusion into a group. For Paul and Barnabas to be offered this by Peter, James, and John meant that the disciples recognized and affirmed their leadership as ministers of the gospel of Jesus. This was important because Paul and Barnabas were not among the original twelve disciples of Jesus. Paul also had a reputation as one who had been persecuting Christians.[1] Even though God had charted a new and better future for Paul, sometimes his pesky past was hard to forget.

What are some things you regret that are hard to forget in your pesky past?

Sometimes, our past is a weapon the enemy uses against us to paralyze us from moving forward.

God has power over our past. Peter, James, and John recognized God's transforming power in Paul. Sometimes, our past is a weapon the enemy uses against us to paralyze us from moving forward. We can get caught in cycles of thinking that we are unworthy of God's goodness, that we are bad decision-makers and can't trust our current decisions, or even that we cannot escape the consequences of our mistakes we must live with. Even Paul, whom God used in mighty ways to plant countless new churches, proclaim the gospel, perform miracles, and author much of the New Testament, had a sinful past. But God kept him thinking and moving forward. That is what God wants for you too.

Read these four verses to help you let go of past mistakes. Write out the one that speaks most deeply to you today.

- Isaiah 43:18-19
- 2 Corinthians 5:17
- Job 17:9
- Philippians 3:13-14

You are not your past. Let me just say that again: you are not your past. Say it with me: I am not my past.

You are not your past. Let me just say that again: **you are not your past**. Say it with me: **I am not my past**.

Our past can inform our future, but our past mistakes are not held against us before God when we confess them, turn away from our sin (what the Bible calls repentance), and try to chart a new course honoring Jesus.

These ministry leaders—Peter, James, John, Paul, and Barnabas—were all perfectly flawed, just like you and me. But they were faithful. *Intentionally* faithful to the call that God put on their lives. They were strategic. Peter, James, and John stayed in the lane of working primarily with the Jews, and Paul and Barnabas stayed in the lane of working with the Gentiles.

What did Peter, James, and John highlight as important for Paul and Barnabas to do in their ministry as they worked with the Gentiles? (Hint: Galatians 2:10)

Read what Jesus said about how we should interact with the poor:

- Luke 14:12-14   • Luke 16:19-25

Here are a few other verses from the Old Testament:

- Proverbs 14:21   • Proverbs 28:27

How do you interact with the poor? Take a few minutes to ask God and listen to Him about what He may want you to do. Write your response below.

Our last encounter of Peter interacting with Paul is found in Galatians 2. Paul and Peter both ended up in Antioch and had a tense moment. Antioch was a prominent city in ancient Syria and is now a central town called Antakya in south-central Turkey.

Followers of Jesus Christ were first labeled "Christians" in Antioch (Acts 11:26). Actually, this was an insult; the term was used in a derogatory way.[2] They were Christ-followers, and Christ had been executed. Even though it was not seen as a positive word, we should note that the group had grown so significantly large that a word was needed to describe them.[3]

Read Galatians 2:11-16. What did Paul do to Peter when Peter came to Antioch?

What did Paul say Peter used to do?

But that had changed. What did Paul say that Peter had begun to do?

What did Paul say was Peter's motivation for this change?

We are back to the circumcision issue again. It is hard for us to understand what a big deal this was in their context. Since the time that Jews were asked to begin the practice of circumcision, they knew this as a mark that set them apart from the rest of the world.[4] It physically distinguished them as God's people.

Read the backstory of what God commanded Abraham about circumcision in Genesis 17:10-14. What do you notice?

According to the Bible's chronology, Abraham lived in the eighteenth-century BC. That was thirty-eight hundred years before Christ was born. That is a lot of history. Every male Jewish baby born would be circumcised with a sharp flint knife (Joshua 5:2) on the eighth day of their life. The foreskin of their penis would be cut.

Today, scientists tell us there can be some health benefits to being circumcised, such as fewer urinary tract infections in their first year of life. Circumcision makes hygiene easier. It does not affect sexual function or fertility.[5]

Sometimes, skeptics ask if God created the foreskin just to be removed. Perhaps God was focused on continually putting reminders in front of people that following the ways of God requires sacrifice, commitment, and separation from the ways of the world. The small amount of blood shed in circumcision was a constant reminder that life was in the blood. Life was to be honored. Blood was special because life is special.[6]

How would anyone know if you were a circumcised male? Someone could simply ask. If you chose to lie, the truth would soon become apparent, as everyday tasks such as bathing and other toiletries were not always done in complete privacy. Eventually, someone would notice.[7]

As crucial as this faith-honoring cultural norm was for the Jews, something happened that was even more important. Jesus was pierced on a cross for all people—for Jews and Gentiles, for men and women, for slaves and free (Galatians 3:28).

Jesus shed his precious lifeblood to cover all of us with forgiveness for our sins. This is called atonement. Jesus suffered the penalty for our sins when He died on the cross. He did this with great love and compassion for humanity so that our sins could be removed from each of us. This is what the gift of grace is. We did not deserve it, but Jesus's love for us compelled Him.

His love was so great that He wanted to make this incredible, ultimate sacrifice so that we could be in a relationship with a holy, pure God, who could not stand sin. Now, when God looks at those who have believed in their heart and confess with their mouth that Jesus is Lord and the one who saves us, God sees Jesus's sacrifice covering all our wrongdoings.

Jesus never sinned, making Him the only one who could ever be this powerful sacrifice for everyone else (2 Corinthians 5:21). The resurrection of Jesus proved Him to be a conqueror over both sin and death. They don't get to win the day. Not today, Satan.

No longer was circumcision necessary. Paul was determined that this message must supersede the tradition of circumcision, which was the defining mark of God's people. Now Jesus was the defining mark of God's people—all of them.[8]

Write out Galatians 2:20.

> **Jesus shed his precious lifeblood to cover all of us with forgiveness for our sins.... We did not deserve it, but Jesus's love for us compelled Him.**

Read Galatians 2:21. Why is grace so important for us to hold on to as a primary aspect of faith?

Read Colossians 2:11-12.

Circumcision had been replaced with baptism, an outward symbol of what Christ has done inwardly in the hearts of Christians. In Romans 6:3-4, Paul wrote that baptism is symbolic of dying and being buried with Christ when believers go under the water. Then when they rise from the water, they rise in new life just as Jesus was resurrected from the dead. It is a beautiful and powerful tradition of the church.

Read these verses about baptism:

- **Mark 16:15-16**   • **Acts 2:38**   • **Acts 22:16**

Have you been baptized? What is your baptism story? Is this something you would like to do?

Read Galatians 2:15-16. How does Paul say that Jews are justified? (This is the word Paul used to describe how people are forgiven and made pure before a holy and pure God.)

It is not the _____ but rather _____ that is the most important thing.

Paul doubled down on one thing: faith in Jesus. Faith means that you believe God. You trust Jesus. You are loyal to the Spirit of God.

We don't have Peter's response to Paul's rebuke. Still, I believe Peter must have course-corrected, just as he did many times with Jesus, and continued to preach, heal, and minister in Jesus's name to both Jews and Gentiles (like Cornelius, whom we studied earlier). The forgiving waters for both Jews and Gentiles flow from the living water of Jesus.

Write down what you have learned about faith from Peter in this study.

Where do you need faith in your life today? Faith is a daily decision to surrender to God's authority, power, and will. Jesus walks with us through that journey. The Spirit gives us abilities beyond ourselves to do hard things. Through the Spirit, we can sacrifice our own will and surrender our selfishness to the greater good of God's kingdom. Write below what you are trusting God to do that is beyond your own abilities.

Let's get our worship on with Hillsong United singing "Oceans (Where Feet May Fail)."

WEEK 6 FOCUS VERSE: LEARN IT AND LIVE IT.

Try filling in the blanks to help you learn the verse.

Each of _____ should use whatever _____ you have _____

to _____ others, as _____ _____ of God's

_____ in its _____ forms.

(1 Peter 4:10)

DAY 5: ANCHORS AWEIGH

I used to hate sitting on the bench when I played volleyball and basketball in middle school and high school. I'm only 5'2", so I eventually gave up basketball since everyone seemed to keep growing except for me. But I loved to be in the game. I'd cheer on my teammates from the bench but participating was always better. I still remember games in which I was not performing well, making mistake after mistake or missing opportunities, and the coach would take me out of the game and put someone else in. Ugh. I'd move from the game to the bench, knowing I had made too many mistakes and someone needed to take my place. But here's the thing: no one ever had a perfect game. Even the person who subbed in for me would start making mistakes, and they would need a replacement at some point too.

Remember that: No one is perfect. Not even followers of Jesus Christ.

That's what we've focused on this entire study—being perfectly flawed. Peter models intentional faithfulness despite stumble after stumble. And God loves it. God loves him. God works with it. God works through him.

Peter continued to be faithful, even while flawed. God continued to forgive and build His church. Peter got into trouble all the way to the end. He was perfectly flawed. Just like me. But God still used Him. God kept him in the game, even after every mistake.

I'm so thankful for Peter's life and example. He reminds me that I'm not out of the game even when I make mistakes.

Two New Testament books were authored by Peter: 1 Peter and 2 Peter. There is much New Testament scholarly debate over whether Peter wrote them or someone else did and put his name on them to boost credibility. I'm not sure we'll ever know 100 percent until we get to heaven and sit down for a chat with Peter. But until that day, I like that Peter's name is on the two books, and I love to look for connections between Peter's faith journey with Jesus and the words written in these two books.

No one is perfect. Not even followers of Jesus Christ.

Read 1 Peter 1:1-2. What did Peter call God's people? Check all that apply:

_____ Chosen   _____ Strangers in the world

_____ Elect   _____ Scattered throughout the nations

What did Peter highlight about each part of the Trinity?

God _____

Spirit _____

Jesus _____

Peter spent a lot of his life making decisions that were fear-based, and Jesus continually reached out to him and met him where he was. When Peter got out of the boat to meet Jesus on the water, he did so with faith and courage. But the wind and the waves brought a fresh batch of fear. Jesus extended his hand to Peter immediately on the water and caught him.

> Immediately, Jesus **reached out his hand and caught him**. *"You of little faith,"* he said, *"why did you doubt?"*
>
> *(Matthew 14:31, emphasis added)*

Life ebbs and flows with moments of courage and fear for all of us. Jesus is there through it all.

Read 1 Peter 5:6. When will God's hand lift you when you need it?

Depending on your translation, the word καιρός is translated as "time." It has a range of meanings around time: the right time, the opportune time, the proper time, the appointed time.[1]

As he wrote this, I imagine Peter remembering that hand of Jesus catching him. He could confidently encourage each of us who would come after him in this journey of faith that God is faithful to catch us.

Write out 1 Peter 5:7.

What should we do when we are afraid and anxious? Peter experienced those moments all throughout his life, just as we do. But the student had become the teacher. Maybe the nets he used to cast out into the sea to catch fish swirled in his mind as he encouraged believers to cast big nets of faith. Cast our fears out to Jesus. He can bring abundance out of the dark void that overwhelms us.

> When he had finished speaking, he said to Simon, "Put out into deep water, and let down the nets for a catch." Simon answered, "Master, we've worked hard all night and haven't caught anything. But because you say so, I will let

Cast our fears out to Jesus. He can bring abundance out of the dark void that overwhelms us.

down the nets." When they had done so, they caught such a large number of fish that their nets began to break.

(Luke 5:4-6)

The Bible seems to abruptly stop reporting Peter's story. Its emphasis, of course, is on Jesus and His church, not on Peter's life. We have reports from other historical sources about what happened to Peter.

According to Christian tradition passed down through the ages, Peter was crucified in Rome under Emperor Nero after the Great Fire of Rome in AD 64. It destroyed much of Rome, and Nero blamed the Christians. Church tradition and testimony from many early Christian writers state that Peter was crucified upside down because he did not believe himself worthy to die in the same way that Jesus did.[2]

> Origen (AD 184–253) in his *Commentary on the Book of Genesis III*, quoted by Eusebius of Caesaria in his *Ecclesiastical History (III, 1)*, said: "Peter was crucified at Rome with his head downwards, as he himself had desired to suffer."[3]

> Peter of Alexandria, who was bishop of Alexandria and died around AD 311, wrote an epistle *On Penance*, in which he says: "Peter, the first of the apostles, having been often apprehended and thrown into prison, and treated with ignominy, was last of all crucified at Rome."[4]

> Jerome (AD 327–420) wrote that "at Nero's hands Peter received the crown of martyrdom being nailed to the cross with his head towards the ground and his feet raised on high, asserting that he was unworthy to be crucified in the same manner as his Lord."[5]

There is even an early writing that describes Peter's wife also being martyred, with Peter calling encouragement to her until the end.

> Eusebius cites Clement and claims that St. Peter's wife was martyred shortly before Peter, "They say, accordingly, that when the blessed Peter saw his own wife led out to die, he rejoiced because of her summons and her return home, and called to her very encouragingly and comfortingly, addressing her by name, and saying, 'Oh thou, remember the Lord.'"[6]

Peter is considered the first pope or leader of the church in Rome. The word *pope* is from the Latin *papa*, which means papa or father. The word *pope* was not used until the ninth century, but it was applied to the leaders or bishops of the church of Rome, with Peter being credited as the first leader of the church of Rome.[7]

Many believe that the Gospel of Mark was written by John Mark, who was an assistant to Peter. Thus, Mark's Gospel is traditionally considered closest to Peter's perspective.

Clement of Alexandria, in the fragments of his work Hypotyposes (AD 190) preserved and cited by the historian Eusebius in his Church History (VI, 14:6), writes:

> As Peter had preached the Word publicly at Rome and declared the Gospel by the Spirit, many who were present requested that Mark, who had followed him for a long time and remembered his sayings, should write them out. And having composed the Gospel, he gave it to those who had requested it.

Also, Irenaeus wrote about this tradition:

> After their (Peter and Paul's) passing, Mark also, the disciple and interpreter of Peter, transmitted to us in writing the things preached by Peter.[8]

The Gospel of Mark is written anonymously so we don't know for sure. The early church fathers wrote about the authorship of Mark, and those are the oldest surviving written testimonies of its authorship.[9] We can add it to our list to ask Peter when we sit down with him and have coffee in heaven.

Peter left us a powerful legacy of faith. Flawed. Forgiven. Fervent.

> *And I tell you that **you are Peter, and on this rock, I will build my church**, and the gates of Hades will not overcome it.*
>
> *(Matthew 16:18, emphasis added)*

Peter was the rock that Jesus used to begin a massive construction project that continues today. It is the expansion of hope. Jesus is for every Jew and Gentile, every male and female, and all who are slave or free (Galatians 3:28). Jesus is the cornerstone of the church.

> *Consequently, you are no longer foreigners and strangers but fellow citizens with God's people and **also members of his household, built on the foundation of the apostles and prophets, with Christ Jesus himself as the chief cornerstone.** In him the whole building is joined together and rises to become a holy temple in the Lord. And in him you too are being built together to become a dwelling in which God lives by his Spirit.*
>
> *(Ephesians 2:19-22, emphasis added)*

Let's invite Jesus to keep building His Kingdom here on earth. Worship with Rend Collective singing "Build Your Kingdom."

From Jerusalem to Samaria to the first Gentile conversion with Cornelius, Jesus kept His promise to Peter and built story after story of people who came to know the goodness of a life built on Jesus. With the hope, the power, the truth, and the love that only Jesus has, He calls us to get out of the boat (our old way of doing things) and take every next step with Him—on the water or land—to the ends of the earth. Anchors aweigh, my friends. Anchors aweigh.

*"But you will receive power when the Holy Spirit comes on you; and **you will be my witnesses in Jerusalem, and in all Judea and Samaria, and to the ends of the earth.**"*

(Acts 1:8, emphasis added)

Amen and Amen.

How would you describe Peter to someone who didn't know him?

How has God used this study on Peter to grow your faith?

WEEK 6 FOCUS VERSE: LEARN IT AND LIVE IT.

Try filling in the blanks to help you learn the verse.

Each of _____ should use whatever _____ you have _____ to _____ others, as _____ _____ of God's _____ in its _____ forms.

(1 Peter 4:10)

Perfectly

Flawed...
Forgiven,
and Faithful.

Video Viewer Guide: *Week 6*

Our human instinct is to _____ our flaws so they don't _____ our weaknesses.

The pursuit of human _____ is an unattainable _____.

Focus on what is going _____ rather than what is going _____.

When we walk with Jesus, His _____ becomes ours.

When _____ meets _____, lives change.

By the _____ of God, we find Peter's life redefined.

Discussion Questions: *Week 6*

Think about these questions as you prepare to meet with your small group.

- Read Acts 9:32-43. What stands out to you about the account of Peter with Aeneas and Dorcas (Tabitha)?

- Where have you seen Jesus be your strength when you felt weak?

- What will you remember most about Peter and his journey with Jesus from this study?

- How can you let your flaws be used by God to reveal His strength, power, and glory?

- What is one of the most helpful things God has revealed to you during this six-week study?

perfectly flawed

Share one word with each member of your group that you would use to describe them. Write down the words to encourage each person.

Hey Friend!

It's been great getting to learn more about the apostle Peter… FLAWS & ALL!

Remember that God loves us and chose us, even with all of our imperfections.

Celebrate what God has done in your group through your time together.

- What prayers have been answered?

- Where has God provided direction on next steps?

- Where have you seen God be strong when you felt weak?

- What friendships have been built?

- How have you grown in your faith?

- How has your relationship with Jesus been impacted through the journey with Peter?

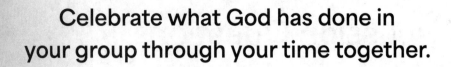

Let's Celebrate!

I'D LOVE TO HEAR FROM YOU!

LiSa ToNeY

I would love to hear from you. What has God been up to in your life throughout this study?

Take a photo of your last answer page and upload it with this QR code or go to **lisatoney.com/peterrocks**.

Please stay in touch on Instagram and Facebook:

LisaToneyLife   LisaToneyLife

Take a photo with your book or small group and post it with these hashtags to share in the joy of our *Perfectly Flawed* community, which is leaning into the transformative power of Jesus to turn our weaknesses into strengths for His glory.

#peterrocks #perfectlyflawed

A Final Word from Peter

His divine power has given us everything we need for a godly life through our knowledge of him who called us by his own glory and goodness. Through these he has given us his very great and precious promises, so that through them you may participate in the divine nature, having escaped the corruption in the world caused by evil desires.

For this very reason, make every effort to add to your faith goodness; and to goodness, knowledge; and to knowledge, self-control; and to self-control, perseverance; and to perseverance, godliness; and to godliness, mutual affection; and to mutual affection, love. For if you possess these qualities in increasing measure, they will keep you from being ineffective and unproductive in your knowledge of our Lord Jesus Christ.

(2 Peter 1:3-8)

But grow in the grace and knowledge of our Lord and Savior Jesus Christ. To him be glory both now and forever! Amen.

(2 Peter 3:18)

A Final Word from Jesus

And I tell you that you are Peter, and on this rock I will build my church, and the gates of Hades will not overcome it.

(Matthew 16:18)

To the ends of the earth!

A Word of Thanks

Thanks for joining me for this study of Peter and Jesus. What an honor to get to walk alongside Peter's journey with Jesus and witness the transformative work of the Holy Spirit in his life. Peter learned that it is not our perfection that defines us but rather our willingness to acknowledge our weaknesses and surrender them to the God. Our imperfections are not obstacles to be overcome, but rather invitations for Jesus to show up in some big ways.

Jesus embraced Peter despite all his shortcomings, modeling that our weaknesses are not what define us in God's eyes. Instead, Jesus writes a beautiful story of restoration and redemption for each one of us. Our flaws make us human. Our imperfections fuel our faith allowing us to surrender our weaknesses to God.

For a God who crafted the universe out of chaos, our imperfections are amazing raw materials waiting to be sculpted into something beautiful. In the hands of God Almighty, our weaknesses can become strengths that we never expected.

As we navigate our own journeys, our imperfections are where God's grace shines most brilliantly, turning our weaknesses into strengths and inviting a deeper connection with Jesus. Our flaws are not barriers to God's plan but rather integral parts of it, for He chooses to work through our imperfections to reveal His perfect will.

So let us acknowledge our flaws with courage and conviction, knowing that in the eyes of a God who sees us as we truly are, we are perfect vessels for His extraordinary grace.

Flawed & Faithful,

Video Viewer Guide: *Answers*

Week 1
disrupt
love | FISH
depth | emptiness |
answer
Jesus
love | disrupts | hope
right relationships
LIVING HOPE
trade | strengths
sin
abundance | emptiness
love | disrupts | hope

Week 2
near | fear
let go | hold on
taking action
paralyzes | mobilizes
towards | meets
haze | gaze
with

Week 3
Pantheism
Man
God
living hope
Anointed One
Anointed One
endure
enough

Week 4
compassion
identity
caved
risen | dead
need
imperfections | used
wastes | pain
abundance

Week 5
ALIVE
each | individually
new harvest
soul
waiting | working
remain
asking | trusting
faithful

Week 6
hide | expose
perfection | direction
right | wrong
strength
compassion | action
goodness

Notes

Week 1 | Day 1: Unfurling the Sails
1. Mishnah Avat 5:21: Stages of Life. Trans. Danby, The Mishnah, p. 458.

Week 1 | Day 2: Unexpected Catch
1. Wilkins, Michael J. *The NIV Application Commentary: Matthew: From Biblical Text to Contemporary Life.* Zondervan, 2004.
2. FJ, Sheed. The Confessions of St. Augustine. 1 e., Vol. 1, New York, Sheed and Ward, 1943. 1 Vols.
3. *St. Augustine's Confessions* (Lib 1,1-2,2.5,5: CSEL 33, 1-5*).

Week 1 | Day 3: Beacon of Hope
1. Wilkins, Michael J. *The NIV Application Commentary: Matthew: From Biblical Text to Contemporary Life.* Zondervan, 2004.
2. "Capernaum-City of Jesus and Its Jewish Synagogue." *Israeli Missions Around The World*, 26 November 2003, https://embassies.gov.il/MFA/IsraelExperience/history/Pages/Capernaum%20-%20City%20of%20Jesus%20and%20its%20Jewish%20Synagogue.aspx. Accessed 4 April 2024.
3. "He Went To Synagogue." *That the World May Know*, https://www.thattheworldmayknow.com/he-went-to-synagogue. Accessed 4 April 2024.
4. Reed, Jonathan L. *Archaeology and the Galilean Jesus: A Re-Examination of the Evidence.* Bloomsbury Academic, 2002.
5. "The House of Peter: The Home of Jesus in Capernaum?" *Biblical Archaeology Society*, 29 March 2011, https://www.biblicalarchaeology.org/daily/biblical-sites-places/biblical-archaeology-sites/the-house-of-peter-the-home-of-jesus-in-capernaum/. Accessed 4 April 2024.
6. Wilkins, *The NIV Application Commentary: Matthew.*

Week 1 | Day 4: Shining Through the Fog
1. Danby, Herbert, translator. *The Mishnah: Translated from the Hebrew with Introduction and Brief Explanatory Notes.* Hendrickson Publishers, 2011. Pirkei Avot 1:4.
2. Brand, Chad, et al., editors. *Holman Illustrated Bible Dictionary.* Education During Bible Times, B&H Publishing Group, 2015.
3. Safrai, Shmuel. *The Jewish People in the First Century.* Vol. 2, Sec 1, p. 953, Brill Academic Pub; Illustrated edition, (January 1, 1988).
4. Strelan, Rick, ed. *Luke the Priest: The Authority of the Author of the Third Gospel*, pp. 102-110, Ashgate Pub. Limited, 2008.
5. "Volume 6 | In the Dust of the Rabbi." That the World May Know, https://www.thattheworldmayknow.com/in-the-dust-of-the-rabbi. Accessed 5 April 2024.
6. Pirkei Avot 1:4, https://www.sefaria.org/English_Explanation_of_Pirkei_Avot.1.4.2?lang=bi
7. Young, Brad H. *Meet the Rabbis: Rabbinic Thought and the Teachings of Jesus.* Baker Publishing Group, 2007.

8. Wilkins, Michael J. *The NIV Application Commentary: Matthew: From Biblical Text to Contemporary Life*. Zondervan, 2004.

Week 1 | Day 5: Healing Voyage

1. Wilkins, Michael J. *The NIV Application Commentary: Matthew: From Biblical Text to Contemporary Life*. Zondervan, 2004.
2. Adler, Cyrus, et al. "HAZZAN—JewishEncyclopedia.com." *Jewish Encyclopedia*, https://www.jewishencyclopedia.com/articles/7426-hazzan. Accessed 5 April 2024.
3. "Synagogues of Jesus' Time." *That the World May Know*, https://www.thattheworldmayknow.com/synagogues-of-jesus-time. Accessed 5 April 2024.
4. Wilkins, *The NIV Application Commentary: Matthew*.

Week 2 | Day 1: Netting Insight

1. Bock, Darrell L. *Luke: The NIV Application Commentary from Biblical Text to Contemporary Life*. Zondervan Publishing House, 1996.
2. Wilkins, Michael J. *The NIV Application Commentary: Matthew: From Biblical Text to Contemporary Life*. Zondervan, 2004.
3. Bock, *Luke: The NIV Application Commentary from Biblical Text to Contemporary Life*.

Week 2 | Day 2: The Crew's Quest

1. "450 Turkish Sheep Leap to Their Deaths." Fox News, 8 July 2005, https://www.foxnews.com/story/450-turkish-sheep-leap-to-their-deaths. Accessed 11 April 2024.
2. Schoenian, Susan. "Sheep 201: Behavior." *Sheep 101*, https://www.sheep101.info/201/behavior.html. Accessed 11 April 2024.
3. Wilkins, Michael J. *The NIV Application Commentary: Matthew: From Biblical Text to Contemporary Life*. Zondervan, 2004.

Week 2 | Day 3: Seas of Plenty

1. Hansen, Collin. "Story Behind | Christian History Magazine." *Christian History Institute*, https://christianhistoryinstitute.org/magazine/article/story-behind. Accessed 24 April 2024.
2. Wilkins, Michael J. *The NIV Application Commentary: Matthew: From Biblical Text to Contemporary Life*. Zondervan, 2004.
3. "Ichthys, The Christian Fish Symbol Origin and History Facts." *Bible Study Tools*, 22 March 2022, https://www.biblestudytools.com/bible-study/topical-studies/the-christian-fish-symbol-origin-and-history-facts.html. Accessed 24 April 2024.
4. "What Should We Know about the Number 12 in the Bible?—Topical Studies." *Bible Study Tools*, 21 December 2023, https://www.biblestudytools.com/bible-study/topical-studies/what-should-we-know-number-12-in-the-bible.html. Accessed 24 April 2024.
5. Wilkins, *The NIV Application Commentary: Matthew*.

Week 2 | Day 4: Course Correction

1. Bruce, Frederick Fyvie. *The International Bible Commentary with the New International Version*. Edited by Frederick Fyvie Bruce, M. Pickering, 1986.
2. Wilkins, Michael J. *The NIV Application Commentary: Matthew: From Biblical Text to Contemporary Life*. Zondervan, 2004.

3.   Wilkins, *The NIV Application Commentary: Matthew.*

4.   Wilkins, *The NIV Application Commentary: Matthew.*

5.   "ἀσύνετος" Free Online Greek Dictionary | billmounce.com." Bill Mounce, https://www.billmounce.com/greek-dictionary/parabole. Accessed August 05, 2024.

Week 2 | Day 5: Charting Compassion

1.   Ryan, Joel. "What Did Jesus Mean When He Said to Forgive "Seventy Times Seven"?" *Christianity.com*, https://www.christianity.com/wiki/sin/what-is-the-significance-of-seventy-times-seven-in-forgiveness.html. Updated August 14, 2024.

2.   G. Connor Salter. "When Jesus said to Forgive "Seventy Times Seven", What Did He Mean?" *Bible Study Tools*, https://www.biblestudytools.com/bible-study/topical-studies/why-is-seventy-times-seven-still-so-radical-today.html. Updated August 14, 2024.

3.   Wilkins, Michael J. *The NIV Application Commentary: Matthew: From Biblical Text to Contemporary Life.* Zondervan, 2004.

4.   Smith, Scotty. "Whether 77 Times or 490 Times, the Call to Forgive Persists." *The Gospel Coalition*, 16 January 2018, https://www.thegospelcoalition.org/blogs/scotty-smith/whether-77-times-490-times-call-forgive-persists/. Accessed 28 April 2024.

Week 3 | Day 1: Netting Wonders

1.   "Free Online Greek Dictionary | billmounce.com." *Bill Mounce*, https://www.billmounce.com/greek-dictionary/protos. Accessed 27 April 2024.

2.   Wilkins, Michael J. *The NIV Application Commentary: Matthew: From Biblical Text to Contemporary Life.* Zondervan, 2004.

3.   "Ruins at Banias—King Herod's Palace Identified at Caesarea Philippi." *Biblical Archaeology Society*, 18 May 2022, https://www.biblicalarchaeology.org/daily/biblical-sites-places/biblical-archaeology-sites/ruins-at-banias-king-herods-palace-identified-at-caesarea-philippi/. Accessed 27 April 2024.

4.   "PAN CULT—Ancient Greek Religion." *Theoi Greek Mythology*, https://www.theoi.com/Cult/PanCult.html. Accessed 27 April 2024.

5.   "Ruins at Banias—King Herod's Palace Identified at Caesarea Philippi."

6.   "Greek word for you (sg)." *Bill Mounce*, https://www.billmounce.com/greekvocabulary/%CF%83%CF%8D. Accessed 27 April 2024.

7.   Wilkins, *The NIV Application Commentary: Matthew.*

8.   Goodrick, Edward W., and John R. Kohlenberger. *The NIV Exhaustive Bible Concordance, Third Edition: A Better Strong's Bible Concordance.* Edited by John R. Kohlenberger, Zondervan, 2015.

9.   "Σατανᾶς" | Free Online Greek Dictionary | billmounce.com.

Week 3 | Day 2: Sunrise

1.   Wilkins, Michael J. *The NIV Application Commentary: Matthew: From Biblical Text to Contemporary Life.* Zondervan, 2004.

2.   Wilkins, *The NIV Application Commentary: Matthew.*

Week 3 | Day 3: Maritime Money

1.   Barclay, William. *The Gospel of Matthew, Volume Two.* Translated by William Barclay, Presbyterian Publishing Corporation, 2017.

2. "Paying Taxes (Matthew 17:24-27 and 22:15-22)." *Theology of Work*. https://www.theologyofwork.org/new-testament/matthew/tales-of-two-kingdoms-matthew-11-17/paying-taxes-matthew-1724-27-and-2215-22/. Accessed 28 April 2024.

3. "The Temple tax—Tyndale Bibles." *Tyndale House Publishers*, https://www.tyndale.com/sites/tyndalebibles/the-temple-tax/. Accessed 28 April 2024.

4. Wilkins, Michael J. *The NIV Application Commentary: Matthew: From Biblical Text to Contemporary Life*. Zondervan, 2004.

5. Hernandez, Dominick. "Why Did the Son of God Pay the Temple Tax?" *Biola University*, 4 October 2021, https://www.biola.edu/blogs/good-book-blog/2021/why-did-the-son-of-god-pay-the-temple-tax. Accessed April 28, 2024.

6. Hernandez, "Why Did the Son of God Pay the Temple Tax?"

7. Hernandez, "Why Did the Son of God Pay the Temple Tax?"

Week 3 | Day 4: Treasure Trove

1. Wilkins, Michael J. *The NIV Application Commentary: Matthew: From Biblical Text to Contemporary Life*. Zondervan, 2004.

Week 3 | Day 5: Fisherman's Harvest

1. Wilkins, Michael J. *The NIV Application Commentary: Matthew: From Biblical Text to Contemporary Life*. Zondervan, 2004.

2. "Fig Facts: Enchanting Facts about Figs." *Valley Fig Growers*, https://valleyfig.com/our-story/fig-facts/. Accessed April 27, 2024.

3. "Fig Trees." *BiblePlaces.com*, https://www.bibleplaces.com/fig-trees/. Accessed April 27, 2024.

Week 4 | Day 1: Navigating New Horizons

1. Lemos, T. M. "Did the Ancient Israelites Think Children Were People?" *Biblical Archaeology Society*, 2 March 2023, https://www.biblicalarchaeology.org/daily/biblical-topics/bible-interpretation/ancient-israel-children-personhood/. Accessed 8 May 2024.

2. Wilkins, Michael J. *The NIV Application Commentary: Matthew: From Biblical Text to Contemporary Life*. Zondervan, 2004.

3. Goodrick, Edward W., and John R. Kohlenberger. *The NIV Exhaustive Bible Concordance, Third Edition: A Better Strong's Bible Concordance*. Edited by John R. Kohlenberger, Zondervan, 2015.

4. "Josephus on the Essenes." *Biblical Archaeology Society*, 9 June 2022, https://www.biblicalarchaeology.org/daily/biblical-artifacts/dead-sea-scrolls/josephus-on-the-essenes/. Accessed 7 May 2024.

5. Goodrick and Kohlenberger. *The NIV Exhaustive Bible Concordance, Third Edition*.

6. Wilkins, *The NIV Application Commentary: Matthew*.

Week 4 | Day 2: Anchored in Love

1. Burge, Gary M. *The NIV Application Commentary: John: From Biblical Text to Contemporary Life*. Zondervan, 2000.

2. Burge, *The NIV Application Commentary*.

3. Goodrick, Edward W., and John R. Kohlenberger. *The NIV Exhaustive Bible Concordance, Third Edition: A Better Strong's Bible Concordance*. Edited by John R. Kohlenberger, Zondervan, 2015.

Week 4 | Day 3: Stormy Seas

1. Wilkins, Michael J. *The NIV Application Commentary: Matthew: From Biblical Text to Contemporary Life*. Zondervan, 2004.
2. Goodrick, Edward W. and John R. Kohlenberger. *The NIV Exhaustive Bible Concordance, Third Edition: A Better Strong's Bible Concordance*. Edited by John R. Kohlenberger, Zondervan, 2015.
3. Garland, David E. *The NIV Application Commentary: Mark: From Biblical Text to Contemporary Life*. Zondervan, 1996.
4. Garland, *The NIV Application Commentary: Mark*.
5. Garland, *The NIV Application Commentary: Mark*.

Week 4 | Day 4: Tides of Treachery

1. Wikipedia, https://en.wikipedia.org/wiki/Robert_Hanssen. Accessed 1 June 2024.
2. https://www.fbi.gov/history/famous-cases/robert-hanssen. Accessed 1 June 2024.
3. https://www.fbi.gov/history/famous-cases/robert-hanssen.
4. Wikipedia.
5. Wikipedia.
6. Bock, Darrell L. *The NIV Application Commentary: Luke: From Biblical Text to Contemporary Life*. Zondervan, 1996.

Week 4 | Day 5: Wave of Rejuvenation

1. Burge, Gary M. *The NIV Application Commentary: John: From Biblical Text to Contemporary Life*. Zondervan, 2000.
2. Burge, *The NIV Application Commentary: John*.
3. Burge, *The NIV Application Commentary: John*.
4. Burge, *The NIV Application Commentary: John*.

Week 5 | Day 1: A Breath of Fresh Air

1. Fernando, Ajith. *The NIV Application Commentary: Acts: From Biblical Text to Contemporary Life*. Zondervan, 1998.
2. Marini, Irmo. *Psychosocial Aspects of Disability: Insider Perspectives and Strategies for Counselors*. Chapter 1, p. 5, Springer Publishing Company, 2017.
3. Miller, M. "The Temple of Jerusalem." *Jerusalem-Insiders-Guide.com*, https://www.jerusalem-insiders-guide.com /temple-of-jerusalem.html. Accessed 2 March 2024.
4. Caldecott, W. Shaw. "Gate, The Beautiful Meaning—Bible Definition and References." *Bible Study Tools*, https://www.biblestudytools.com/dictionary/gate-the-beautiful/#google_vignette. Accessed March 2, 2024.
5. "Strong's Greek: 1813. ἐξαλείφω (exaleiphó)—to wipe out, erase, obliterate." BibleApps.com, https://bibleapps.com/greek/1813.htm. Accessed March 2, 2024.

Week 5 | Day 2: Casting Authority

1. Fernando, Ajith. *The NIV Application Commentary: Acts: From Biblical Text to Contemporary Life*. Zondervan, 1998.
2. Antiquities l. 20. c. 8. sect. 7.
3. Fernando, *The NIV Application Commentary: Acts*.
4. Kodashim, Middoth, ch. I, 1-5.
5. Fernando, *The NIV Application Commentary: Acts*.

6. "World Watch List 2024 · Serving Persecuted Christians Worldwide." *Open Doors*, https://www.opendoorsus.org /en-US/persecution/countries/. Accessed 15 March 2024.

Week 5 | Day 3: Hooked on Possibility

1. Fernando, Ajith. *The NIV Application Commentary: Acts: From Biblical Text to Contemporary Life*. Zondervan, 1998.
2. Fernando, *The NIV Application Commentary: Acts*.

Week 5 | Day 4: Tides of Resilience

1. Barker, Kenneth L., and John R. Kohlenberger. *Expositor's Bible Commentary*. Edited by Verlyn D. Verbrugge and Richard P. Polcyn, Zondervan, 2004. Accessed 23 March 2024.
2. Fernando, Ajith. *The NIV Application Commentary: Acts: From Biblical Text To Contemporary Life*. Zondervan, 1998.
3. Zondervan. *Zondervan Illustrated Bible Backgrounds Commentary: Acts Volume 2B*. Edited by Clinton E. Arnold, Zondervan, 2019. Accessed 22 March 2024.
4. Fernando, *The NIV Application Commentary: Acts*.
5. Fernando, *The NIV Application Commentary: Acts*.

Week 5 | Day 5: Depths of Fortitude

1. Cresswell, Julia. *Oxford Dictionary of Word Origins*. Oxford University Press, 2021.
2. "Strong's #4592: *semeion*—Greek/Hebrew Definitions." *Bible Tools*, https://www.bibletools.org/index.cfm /fuseaction/Lexicon.show/ID/G4592/semeion.htm. Accessed 29 March 2024.
3. Fernando, Ajith. *The NIV Application Commentary: Acts: From Biblical Text to Contemporary Life*. Zondervan, 1998.
4. Goodrick, Edward W., and John R. Kohlenberger. *The NIV Exhaustive Bible Concordance, Third Edition: A Better Strong's Bible Concordance*. Edited by John R. Kohlenberger, Zondervan, 2015.
5. "Strong's #5387: *nasiy'*—Greek/Hebrew Definitions." *Bible Tools*, https://www.bibletools.org/index.cfm /fuseaction/lexicon.show/ID/h5387/page/1. Accessed 9 August 2024.
6. "Flogging." *Jewish Virtual Library*, https://www.jewishvirtuallibrary.org/flogging. Accessed 4 April 2024.

Week 6 | Day 1: In the Same Boat

1. Fernando, Ajith. *The NIV Application Commentary: Acts: From Biblical Text to Contemporary Life*. Zondervan, 1998.
2. Eusebius, On the Martyrs of Palestine.
3. https://www.blueletterbible.org/lexicon/g1611/niv/mgnt/0-1/. Accessed June 1, 2024.
4. Thayer, Joseph Henry, et al. *Thayer's Greek-English Lexicon of the New Testament: Coded with Strong's Concordance Numbers*. Edited by Joseph Henry Thayer, translated by Joseph Henry Thayer, Hendrickson, 1996.
5. Fernando, *The NIV Application Commentary: Acts*.

Week 6 | Day 2: Catch and Release

1. "Strong's Greek: 993. Βοανεργές (Boanérges)—Boanerges, an epithet applied to the two sons of Zebedee." *Bible Hub*, https://biblehub.com/greek/993.htm. Accessed February 29, 2024.
2. Black, Carl Clifton. *Mark: Images of an Apostolic Interpreter (Studies on Personalities of the New Testament)*. University of South Carolina Press, 1994. Accessed February 29, 2024.

3. Fernando, Ajith. *The NIV Application Commentary: Acts: From Biblical Text to Contemporary Life*. Zondervan, 1998.

4. Black, *Mark: Images of an Apostolic Interpreter*.

5. "Mary, mother of John Mark." *Wikipedia*, https://en.wikipedia.org/wiki/Mary,_mother_of_John_Mark#/media /File:St._Mark_Syriac_inscription.jpeg. Accessed 29 February 2024.

Week 6 | Day 3: Tangled Lines

1. "The Early Life and Background of Paul, the Apostle." *American Journal of Biblical Theology*. https://www .biblicaltheology.com/Research/WallaceQ01.html. Accessed 29 February 2024.

2. Fernando, Ajith. *The NIV Application Commentary: Acts: From Biblical Text to Contemporary Life*. Zondervan, 1998.

3. Fernando, *The NIV Application Commentary: Acts*.

4. "The Early Life and Background of Paul, the Apostle."

Week 6 | Day 4: Parallel Waters

1. Fernando, Ajith. *The NIV Application Commentary: Acts: From Biblical Text to Contemporary Life*. Zondervan, 1998.

2. Fernando, *The NIV Application Commentary: Acts*.

3. Fernando, *The NIV Application Commentary: Acts*.

4. "Newborn Male Circumcision." *ACOG*, https://www.acog.org/womens-health/faqs/newborn-male-circumcision. Accessed 1 March 2024.

5. Collier, Roger. "Vital or vestigial? The foreskin has its fans and foes." NCBI, https//www.ncbi.nlm.nih.gov/pmc /articles/PM3225416/. Accessed 1 March 2024.

6. Collier, "Vital or vestigial?"

7. Collier, "Vital or vestigial?"

8. Fernando, *The NIV Application Commentary: Acts*.

Week 6 | Day 5: Anchors Aweigh

1. "καιρός | Free Online Greek Dictionary | billmounce.com." *Bill Mounce*, https://www.billmounce.com/greek -dictionary/kairos. Accessed March 1, 2024.

2. Clement of Alexandria. *Hypotyposes*. Preserved and cited by historian Eusebius in Church History (VI, 14:6), AD 190.

3. Eusebius, Church History III.31.

4. Peter of Alexandria. *Canonical Epistle on Penitence Canon 9*.

5. Jerome, Saint. *De Viris Illustribus (On Illustrious Men)*. Chapter 1.

6. Clement of Alexandria.

7. "Pope | Definition, Title, List of Popes, & Facts." *Britannica*, 19 February 2024, https://www.britannica.com/ topic/pope. Accessed March 1, 2024.

8. Donaldson, James. *Ante-Nicene Christian Library: Translations of the Writing of the Fathers Down to AD 325*. Edited by Alexander Roberts, translated by Stramata book 7, ch. 11, vol. 12 p. 451.

9. Donaldson, *Ante-Nicene Christian Library: Translations of the Writing of the Fathers Down to AD 325*.

Watch videos based on *Perfectly Flawed: God Transforms Our Weaknesses into Strengths* with Lisa Toney through Amplify Media.

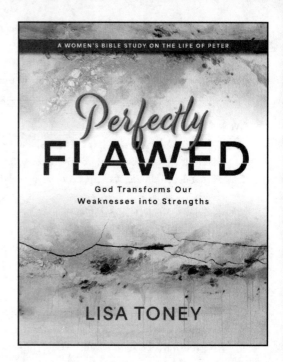

A WOMEN'S BIBLE STUDY ON THE LIFE OF PETER

Perfectly **FLAWED**

God Transforms Our
Weaknesses into Strengths

LISA TONEY

Amplify Media is a multimedia platform that delivers high-quality, searchable content with an emphasis on Wesleyan perspectives for churchwide, group, or individual use on any device at any time. In a world of sometimes overwhelming choices, Amplify gives church leaders and congregants media capabilities that are contemporary, relevant, effective, and, most important, affordable and sustainable.

With *Amplify Media* church leaders can:

- Provide a reliable source of Christian content through a Wesleyan lens for teaching, training, and inspiration in a customizable library
- Deliver their own preaching and worship content in a way the congregation knows and appreciates
- Build the church's capacity to innovate with engaging content and accessible technology
- Equip the congregation to better understand the Bible and its application
- Deepen discipleship beyond the church walls

Ask your group leader or pastor about Amplify Media
and sign up today at www.AmplifyMedia.com.